THE STARS THAT NEVER SHINE

Making of a NFL football player

BY: JOSEPH A. HARRIS

J & J PUBLISHING

ATLANTA * NEW YORK * NORTH CAROLINA * LOS ANGELES

To: Danye
Peace
Stay Blessed,
Joe Harris
#51
L.A. RAMS
Super Bowl
#14

THE STARS THAT NEVER SHINE

(The Making of a SUPERBOWL Football Player)

BY: JOSEPH A. HARRIS

Literary Consultant- Aduke Aremu, Dove LLC
Proof Reader- Dawn Alli
Technical Assistant- Cherice Kirkland

ndove@hotmail.com

Published in the United States of America by
J & J Publishing., Atlanta, Georgia.
ISBN 978-0-9800518-4-1 a trade paperback book.

For book orders, author appearance inquiries
and interviews, contact the Publisher at:
(770) 363 5457

Joseph Harris
Joeharris51@hotmail.com
Library of Congress Cataloging In Publication Data

This publication states the events that occurred from my personal point of view. The purpose of this document is not to malign or discredit any individual or organization. It has been written primarily for the purpose of a "teaching tool" with historic significance from my perspective.

Second Revised Edition

FORWARD

The reason for my writing this book is to inform the youth of our era,
not only how to go about becoming professional athletes, but to prepare
that athlete and his/her support group with information on the world
of football so they can reach their desired goal. This book was written
to help all athletes be it basketball, football, track or whatever the
desired profession is, to brace themselves to be ready to face the
realities of a sports career and life.

I would like to consider this book a tool of necessity.
It is a positive overlook on the day to day challenges that life brings
our way.

The up and coming qualified athletes, who might pursue a career in
the professional field of their choice, should be aware of the obstacles
which might come into play. Mainly, this book should be viewed as an
educational tool to educate not only the athletes, but their family
members who are in their lives to give them support.

First of all, if an athlete is skilled enough to become a professional
then they should understand the pros and the cons of an existing
professional athlete.

Although the media has placed into our minds that the life of a
professional athlete is filled with "Stars" and a life filled with no
clouds: my book offers a more vivid outlook on the real version of what
The media has neglected to explain.

Dreams can come true if a person works hard and diligently to strive to
make their dreams a reality. This opportunity to make our dreams
come true requires a lot of hard work, great mentors and the power of
the Almighty God.

Sincerely,

Joseph "Joe" Harris

Dedication

This book is dedicated to my family......

ACKNOWLEDGEMENTS

Special thanks to Shawna D. Lytle, Claudia McRae and Arthur Roberson who encouraged me to write the book initially and provided invaluable editing advice and feedback. My accountant and long time friend, Luther Harris, who recently died. Literary Consultant and recommendations also came from Aduke Aremu, CEO-Dove LLC and Dove Inc.,Dawn Alli, and Cherice Kirkland.

Special thanks also to Carl Agard-Adelphia Publishing and Media Group for publishing consultation.

Without these individuals' steadfast belief in my story: the book would not have become a "Reality."

Sincerely,

Joseph "Joe" Harris

Prologue
MY CAREER

After graduating from high school, I received a scholarship and went to Georgia Institute of Technology in Atlanta, Ga. and later became one of many to be inducted into the Georgia Institute of Technology Hall of Fame in the year 2000. That was one of my profound achievements.

I currently hold the record for making the most tackles in one season. Also I'm now ranked as #5 in my career.

After graduating from Georgia Institute of Technology with a degree in business, the Chicago Bears then drafted me in the seventh round, in 1974.

Also drafted that year was the great legendary Walter "Sweetness" Payton! He was drafted in the first round. I played for only one year with the Bears.

I then moved to Ontario, Canada to play for the Hamilton Tiger Cats. There I played for two years with one of the fastest players in Canada, out of Dallas, Texas named Dave Shaw. I was captain of the team!

While playing with that team, I would go to Texas each summer to work out with Dave and Hollywood Henderson.

The coach for the Tiger Cats was an astounding man by the name of Bob Shaw who was known for his intimidation and toughness.

From there, I was recruited by the Washington Red Skins by Coach George Allen. He was the head coach back then in 1977. He had chosen two players out of Canada to come back to the N. F. L. from the Canadian league. The other player was Joe Theisman, quarterback for the Toronto Argonauts.

After playing for one year, I was headed to California to complete the promises that I had made to my mom and to myself.

Pete McCullough was one of the coaches with the Washington Red Skins and landed the position of head coach for the San Francisco 49ers. He decided that I was what they needed to complete their defensive line and took me with him.

I was captain of this team as well.

On this team I had the honor of playing with wonderful players such as, Willie Harper, Archie Reese, Freddie Solomon, Cedric Hardeman, Al Collins and The Juice, 0. J. Simpson for the next year and a half.

I moved again to Minnesota to play for the Vikings under Coach Bud Grant for only one year.

Bud Grant was one of the mildest mannered coaches that I ever had the opportunity to play for. He never cursed!

He refused to let any of the players wear sweaters or any warming garments under their uniforms. He felt that it was psychological for the opposing team to see his players in 20- degree weather with no sleeves. This was remarkable to the other teams!

I played with legends like Chuck Munsey, Jim Marshall, Ted Brown, Mac Blair, Fred McNeil and Nat Wright!

I left Minnesota before the season was over, when they brought back a veteran player by the name of Paul Krause. They put me on a waver wire. I was then, picked up by the Los Angeles Rams.

Bud Carson, who recruited me at Georgia Tech, was the defensive coordinator for the Rams. His notoriety was that he built the steel curtain for the Pittsburg Steelers. He and Ray Malovasi, head coach for the Los Angeles Rams said "bring Joe Harris back to California!"

I stayed with the Rams from 1978 to 1983. Playing with distinguishing players like Drew Hill, Mel Owens, Kent

Hill, Wendell Tyler, Billy Waddy, Cullen Bryant, Pat Hadden,and Jack Youngblood.

I also played with Fred Dryer, Pat Thomas, Rod Perry, Phil Murphy, Jackie Slater, Dennis Harrah, Lawrence McCluchen, Ron Jesse, Preston Denard, Eddie Hill, Bob Lee, Frank Carrel, Larry Brooks, George Andrews, Greg Westbrooks and Hacksaw Reynolds.

I moved to Miami to play with Dan Marino, Don Bussillieu and Wally Kildenburg for the Dolphins. Coach Don Shuler headed us for yet again, one year. I'll explain later why I was traded so many times.

Next it was on to Baltimore to play for the Colts. I played with the Colts for less than a year when I was traded again!

This time my career landed me back in Washington, D. C. to play in the league known as the U. S. F. L. (U. S. Football League) and there I played for the Washington Federals.

My last and final professional team in which I played was the Memphis Showboats located in Memphis, Tennessee.

During my entire career, I scored several touchdowns, by way of recovering fumbles.

I was blessed with the skills and ability to play in Super Bowl XIV. It was a great experience, although we, the Rams, lost against the Pittsburg Steelers, 31 to 19. I had the honor of being the Special Team Captain!

As you can see, stability is not something that you should expect as a professional football player.

I will get into the depth of what the "real" glorified

N. F. L. is truly about later in this book. I will also explain why I was traded so many times and hopefully you will understand what and why the role of "politics" is so profound in professional football.

You will see that it is not all that it is cracked up to be and is exploited by the media.

IN THE BEGINNING

Many years ago, in a very small town called Apex, North Carolina, there was a share cropper by the name of, Joseph Alston. The story begins between Apex and Fayetteville, North Carolina. Fayetteville was located just outside of Chapel Hill, North Carolina.

Joseph Alston was a good-looking man. People often mistakenly thought that he was of the Caucasian race, but actually, he was half-Native American and African American. I remember him laughing about the situation. People had a lot of respect for him.

He and his wife bore three boys and one daughter. That one daughter was my mother, Mattie Mae Alston. I didn't really get to know many of my father's family. They weren't around much and me being the quiet child, I never questioned why. I just figured that if I was to know, then they would explain. It really didn't matter much to me anyway.

My grandfather owned one hundred and twenty six acres of farmland. On the farm they grew tobacco, collard greens, corn and green beans. They also had lots of livestock, cows, goats and beautiful horses. That's what I remember most, the beautiful horses.

On the farm, they had all kinds of people working. There were African American people, Native American, as well as white people. Not only did they work the land, but they lived on it too.

My grandfather was a very religious man and he had a head full of beautiful hair. Tall and slender with a pair of the most gorgeous eyes that ever was created.

He would sit all day sometimes listening to the famous Reverend Ike and Oral Roberts. He would send money to support them every week. This is what I now know to be the paying of tithes.

I really didn't understand this back then, but now I do. He instilled in me the desire to be a strong man and to do all of the right things, such as listen to your mother, and abide by the rules of life.

I guess that is what made me the very man that I am today.

One cousin, Richard, ran moonshine throughout the winding roads of the county. I remember that he could drive his tail off. He could drive faster backwards, than most people could drive forward.

He had friends like the family of the great race car driver, Richard Petty. They too ran moonshine all through the winding roads of North Carolina and it was a race to the fullest. My uncle won most of the time and sometimes had to drive in reverse.

My uncle used to tell me stories about how the police would "hem him up in a corner" and he would back the car up so fast, to elude them. He was definitely a bragging kind of man. The stories would captivate me as young boy.

I used to admire the strength of my uncles. I would stare at their muscles in disbelief. They acquired their strength by working very hard on the farm.

MY BIRTH

My mother was visiting some family members in a little town called Pittsboro, North Carolina, located between the cities of Fayetteville, and Apex. (Fayetteville was where I grew up at). While on her travel, she went into labor with me, Joseph Alexander Harris.

On December 6th, 1952, very early in the morning, my mom went into labor, in the middle of town-square. On the left side of a building just off the town-square, was a doctor's office. This is where my mother gave birth to me.

During slavery, it was right in that center building of Apex that they would buy and sell slaves. It is a historical site today.

I grew up on the farm that my grandfather owned. The house that we lived in would be considered small today but back then, it was a pretty good sized house.

My mother was a very strong willed woman. She was a beautiful black woman with long, black straight hair. She had one of the most pleasant smiles that you could possibly imagine and a very loving and giving woman as well.

As you can envision she was gorgeous. I guess the quarter part of Native American in her made her features bold and expressive.

My mother married James Harris at a very young age. He was an army man, and one of the best chefs to ever enlist into the army.

He stood about five feet ten inches tall and was a stern built man with somewhat of a violent temper. He often drank alcohol heavy and that's when his temper would flair.

Between the two of them, they had three boys and one girl, Claretta. One of the boys was John, our half brother, born outside of our family. John lived with my grandfather and died at a very young age in a motorcycle accident. He was extremely energetic and loved to play baseball.

Then there was James, Raymond, and I. Claretta was born between James and me. Outside of their marriage, my father had one child before he married my mom.

We were very close as siblings to say the least. Although we had our arguments, like all siblings do, we loved each other very much.

Our house was quite small. It had a total of only five rooms and with five people living in it. We were somewhat crunched.

My brother and I slept in the same bed, in the same room, with our sister on a roll out bed. Our parents had the other bedroom.

There was the kitchen, living room and bathroom. This pretty much, sums up what it was like growing up in a rural city with parents that were kind of young. There was not a whole lot of money, raising three children.

I didn't really know many of my father's family. I grew up knowing all of my mother's people. As I said, my father was unlike most. He was a good man, although, he had a history of a lifestyle that was somewhat mysterious.

I remember my grandfather would have the farm hands paint the little house every summer. They would keep the grounds nice and neat.

My grandmother, Savannah Alston, had a beautiful garden just outside the front door that extended down the walkway to the road. There she grew azaleas and lilies.

Working on the farm, we would earn $6.00 between my cousin Ed and me. We were best buddies.

We would take that little money and buy things from my granddad's store, which was located in the very house where I grew up. He would have candy, sodas and beers for the workers. It was about five miles to town where the nearest public store was.

All of my uncles would always say that I would someday grow up to be someone special and successful because I loved to run.

I would run through the woods, five miles to the store and pass by the old men out front playing checkers and they would also comment that I would make it someday successfully. They would say, "Look at the boy run!"

GROWING UP

As a young child growing up in a small town, there wasn't a lot to do to occupy oneself. So, we relied on each other to pass the time away.

There were six of us; we called it our little gang. There was Arnell McSwain, William Henry Dobbins, Terrance Murchison, Ronnie McDonald, and the Virgil boys.

All six of us were the best of friends. However, if you were caught walking alone late at night in the path, the same five boys that we called our friends would rob you. They would take whatever you had in your pockets and be laughing at the same time.

When we returned home, and my father found out that we were robbed, he would make us go back and take whatever was stolen from us. He would tell us to take a stick or a brick or something, and that we were not to return home until we retrieved whatever was taken.

It was hard living in the country on a farm in the summer, but it made us tough and strong. This prepared us for the tough world in which we live in now as adults.

My big brother, James, would not let us play with them during the week in the field. The little boys could only play on the weekends.

I vividly remember my big brother running me home, unable to catch me. He ran me home because I was giving him a fighting tough time and because we wanted to play on the field.

I ran as fast as I could and he didn't even "come close" to catching me. That day in particular, I was determined to stand my ground and play on that field no matter what he said.

The gentlemen sitting in front of the local store laughed at my brother and told him that he was fighting a losing battle if he thought that he could catch me. This made my brother even madder.

It wasn't too long after my stance against my big brother, that they let the little guys play on days other then the weekends. We were allowed to play whenever we wanted to after that day. They soon found out that sometimes, little boys could be big boys.

I say that because, it's not the age or size of a person that determines his or her skills. It's the individual striving towards their goals to achieve.

If someone wants something bad enough, they will work extra hard, harder than the next guy, because of their determination: that kind of goes around in a circle, if you know what I mean.

This was a tough pill for the big boys to swallow, but none the less, we earned the respect that was due to us.

This enabled us to learn from watching the big boys. The little boys could only play on the side and we would sometimes play a little football in the street. When the big boys were gone, we would carry on and play a game on the field amongst ourselves.

My strongest memories growing up are intertwined with those of my beloved brother John. He was my oldest brother who was very outgoing and always the life of the party. He had something to say to everyone, and everyone would get something out of what he would say! Everybody loved to talk to him. He was very energetic in his conversing and that thrilled everyone.

He always had words of encouragement and leaned hard on the fact that everyone should treat everyone the same, no matter how rich or how poor, how ugly or how cute they might be.

The adults in the neighborhood admired him for his knowledge and wisdom at such a young age.

This stands out vividly in my memories of John.

John McDean was one of our neighbors and he had a basketball hoop set up in front of his house, it was sort of a park type atmosphere.

Lots of times, we would go out into the darkest of night and shoot the basketball into the hoop in pitch-blackness.

We felt proud to be able to do that without missing. But I would love to pick up that football.

Actually, I thought that basketball would have been my profession, but as it turns out, football took the glory that I had.

My skills were exceptional in both sports in many ways, but football was the successor of the two. I knew that I wanted to become a professional football player when I was as young as twelve years old.

I ran track, which I felt would aid in my endurance. This practice in all three sports gave me great maneuverability that conditioned my technique as well as conditioned me physically for the ultimate game of football.

My development was on going as I prepared myself for the game of football. I'll go into conditioning later on in this book.

One day I had the football and I was running and I ran right into the guy that tried to stop me. His name was Walter Boone. It was then that I realized how much I enjoyed the game of football.

After playing the game myself, I then would watch any game that was available for me to see, be it on television or I would beg my mom to take me to any game that she could.

My favorite N. F. L. Football team was The Chicago Bears. Dick Butkus was the most astounding player on any team, so I thought.

Jim Brown was breath taking with his quick feet and cool moves. He was one of the most physical athletes that I had ever known to play on the field. One man could never take him down! He was a running back for the Cleveland Browns.

I remember watching Willie Wood with total amazement. He played strong safety for The Green Bay Packers. Then there was Sam Huff, the linebacker for the team. The amazing Mr. Huff played for the New York Giants.

Of course, I admired John Mackey with his trivial tight end skills. He was in the starting lineup for the Baltimore Colts.

There were many, many more. These were just a few that really stand out in my mind, hey; I was just a little boy!

Although I was at a very young age, I truly understood the game and was totally into the style in which each player had. Every player had a way of carrying out his duty as a teammate and each player posed as a piece of a puzzle.

There were several plays that seemed to be special to me. Don't ask why, but some of the plays had a magical effect on my abilities to grasp the wonders of football.

I began to study the entire concept of football and what it would take to win at the game. Even though I was a young boy, the game of football consumed my every thought.

My father and older brothers found it interesting that I, as a boy could be so filled with the learning aspect of football. And I was! I was content with learning each and every play. Every step that they made on the field, I knew had a purpose.

REFLECTIONS OF PRE-TEENAGE DAYS

I was very quiet as a child and did not like to cause a stir. But I had one incident where we were in line and this guy pushed me and I hit him really hard in the stomach. I then noticed that he couldn't breathe.

It was then that I knew that I was a hard hitter. The teacher made me sit for the rest of the recess period. I'll never forget it. But I felt that I had done nothing wrong, I was just protecting myself.

My father, my brothers and I, were all somewhat quiet people but we did know how to protect ourselves. This was instilled in all of us from my grandfather.

My grandfather was a stern believer in doing the right thing, but at the same time, he taught us to defend ourselves, even if it might be wrong.

My father said that it didn't take a knockdown; drag-out fight to earn respect from your opponent, just one good solid lick would do the trick. He was right.

We went to an elementary school called Newbold Training School. The schools were about ten stories tall and looked just like a large square with lots and lots of windows. It had a small cafeteria in the side of the humongous square.

We had to walk to the school each day and we would walk along the railroad tracks and through the woods to get to it.

I used to fall off of the rail tracks and hurt my ankles. I had fallen so much that today, I still have scars left from those tracks.

My mother was a chef there. She made certain that my friends and I would all have plenty of food to last us through each day.

It was there that I met my best friend. Charlie Baggett, now the offensive wide receiver coach for the University of Washington.

At recess, we would hold races amongst us. Charlie and I would always tie. I knew then that I was a fast runner.

I'll never forget during that time of my life, I had the wonderful opportunity to see and hear the late great Martin Luther King, Jr. speak at a rally.

The college students were working on the local head start program and invited a few of us to go on a ride into Raleigh, North Carolina. I was supposed to go to church but I "snuck" and rode with them.

Hearing the voice of Martin Luther King, Jr., gave me a sense of pride.

The way his voice rang out above all and the words that were spoken made me feel good about being a Black American. During that time in history we as blacks were just starting to be true citizens. I will never forget Dr. King.

At the rally, I had the distinct chance to see the Ku Klux Klan. They had on bright colors and boy oh boy; it was a sight to see. Then all of a sudden, the Klan started chasing me. I ran through the park and they followed. I ran as fast as my legs would carry me behind a bank.

The police were staked out across the park behind a bank. When they heard the commotion the police asked me why I was running and I pointed back and said, "Do you see all those hooded people?"

That was the first time I was on national television. It was also the day that I got my "butt torn up" by my mother for skipping church to go to the rally. That was the one Sunday that she had decided not to attend church for some reason and was watching the news.

There I was, just as bold as daylight, being interviewed by the spokesperson because I was singled out by the Klansmen to chase.

One day, while playing football, a guy named Dent Reader gets the ball and runs. When he ran, I caught him and hit him so hard that I knocked the wind out of him and at the same time, knocked myself out.

It wasn't until we were driving back home, which was about thirty miles away, that I realized who I was. It was the same store that I used to love to run five miles to, which jarred my memory.

There were actually two stores that presided in the city of Fayetteville, one was the candy store and the other was called the juke joint, which as we got older and grew out of the candy stages in life did we frequent.

It had beer and corn liquor for those who preferred the hard stuff. The other store was for your mother's special items for dinner such as bread or milk.

There was a lady named Mrs. Levy who lived a couple of houses up from us and she was head of the church prayer club. She was also the church bandleader.

I was somewhat a part of this also, that is until Mrs. Levy tried to teach me to play the Clarinet. It was soon discovered that I had no musical abilities.

Walter Boone was one of the guys in our little gang. He lived across the street from us and he loved to play the drum. He would keep the whole neighborhood awake at night by playing those drums. He was a part of the band at the church too.

Everybody in our gang wanted to be the leader, as in any other group situation, someone always wants to be the head honcho in charge. That was a role that my boy, Arnell McSwain, wanted, and sometimes claimed!

Growing up as a young teen, all the boys wanted to get the chance to talk with the new girl in town. It was something to have a fresh new face to call your girl.

Oftentimes, we would compete to see who would get the honor of calling such a girl his own. Only it wasn't a competitive sport that we competed at. It was a fight.

The guys would meet in the back yard at a certain time and then the fight would be on. The winner would win the prize.

We used to roller skate down the steep roads to see who could reach the bottom first. I remember falling down the hill while skating and I slid about fifty yards! My skin was completely raw. This didn't stop me. I got right back up and tried it again.

This taught me never to be a quitter and to this day, I still live by that and almost all that was instilled in me as a kid. My siblings and I waited for his dad to leave and then we would get Anthony to give us food and candy or whatever we wanted. He would do it because he was afraid of us bigger guys.

One Christmas I got a B-B- Gun and my father told me not to aim it at anything living, but being the boy that I was, I would go out and shot birds in the back yard when my father wasn't at home. We called this "skeet shooting". But never did I let my father know or he would have beaten my butt.

Growing up in a religious family, we were taught that all life is sacred. But little boys will be little boys, who someday grow to be real men. That was I, Joseph Alexander Harris.

Another Christmas, I woke up and Santa had brought me a brand new set of weights. I was the only kid on the block who had a real set.

We were very blessed to have loving parents who took the time out to fuss at you or to whip you butt.

Our gang would build homemade go-carts from wooden boxes and old tricycle tires.

We would try to see who could build the fanciest one. We used a piece of wood as our brakes. Sometimes they worked and sometimes they didn't.

We would fall down the hill on roller skates, and we had many embarrassing collisions and wrecks on those go-carts.

Growing up in our neighborhood, we had a period of the afternoon in which we called "Happy Hour". Unlike the "Happy Hour" that adult engage, without alcoholic beverages. After all, we were only kids.

There was a little kid who we called the weak one of "our gang". His name was Anthony and his father owned the joint. I must add that I wanted also to become a positive roll model someday and I started early in my life spreading positive thoughts.

People would say that I was crazy and obsessed with body building and conditioning my body at a tender age.

I was very determined to be strong and conditioned. I would challenge the boys in the gang to see who could lift the most weights.

As usual, it was always down to Charlie and me in the end. Although we were always competing with each other, we never let it stand in the way of that strong bond as friends.

Each morning before school, I would lift those weights and try to concentrate on all of my muscles. I would repeat this in the afternoon when I would come home from school and then again before I went to bed at night.

My nickname was "Mr. Muscles", because I looked like Tarzan! You can only imagine what I looked like with all of those muscles and back then, I was really considered short. I finally grew to be 6'1".

I never paid much attention to that nickname but as I look back on my past, I can truly say that I was in great shape and had a very noticeable, great shape.

I must say that I succeeded at reaching one of the goals that I had set, not knowing then, but I now know. I wanted to achieve an almost perfect body and I had it.

I often shared my aspirations and positive thoughts with several of the athletes at E. E Smith Senior High School.

JUNIOR HIGH SCHOOL DAYS

I went to Junior High School at a place called Washington Drive. I had to walk around a highway, a paved road cross the street at the light and through the neighborhood to get to the school. As I would come around a curve in the street, there on the hill was my junior high school, Washington Drive.

The school was a flat roofed, two-story building. It had five sections to it and in the back was a big, open, red clay field. We practiced football in the back field. The gymnasium was located in the front of the school.

Our little gang would travel to and from school, and when we got to the town, some of the crew would go in and steal goods from the stores.

I was always the lookout man, because I knew that if my dad found out that I stole something, he would whip my butt!

As we grew up, we would be sitting around talking about old times, they would say, "We should have let Joe go in and steal some of the time".

But because I refused to steal, they knew that someday I would be someone special.

Henry Dobbins' was a very close and dear friend to me, just as Charlie was, only in a somewhat different manner. I would go to his house and his mom would feed me as though I was her child.

After we finished stealing, we would go to Henry back yard and we would combine all of our goods together and put them in his back yard shed. He had a pretty good size back yard.

We would have hobbies such as putting together model airplanes and cars. My favorite was airplanes.

These are the types of items that they stole and I would still get to play with the stuff just as though I had stolen them. Actually, I was just as guilty as they were; it's called being a party to a crime.

Down the street from my house lived a couple of my cousins named Willie and Obe Ford who were very slim guys.

Willie was one of the best masonry men ever to go through the course at our school. He was a jack of all trades and I was jack of all sports.

They would always come to my house and eat up all of our food. They would walk in the door with a smile on their face but you knew they came to eat.

We were one big happy family.

I met a man who also graduated from E. E. Smith High School many years before I did and he would have become one of the best baseball catchers that there ever was, had he not chosen to stay in Fayetteville to be with a girl that he loved deeply.

He came up to me one day at our practice and he said, "Joe, I hope that you don't do what I did and stay back for the wrong reasons."

This weighed kind of heavy on my mind for a long time. Partly because I had fallen in love with a young lady by the name of Stephanie McKinney.

She was beautiful and very tall, being that she played basketball at E.E. Smith and was a wonderful cheerleader as well. She was one of the smartest students at school.

Later, she went on to go to school at Spellman College in Atlanta, Georgia. Then she went to the military and now she resides somewhere in the islands of Hawaii.

The thoughts never entered my mind to not pursue my dreams, but I did have hopes that if I left, she would wait for my return.

When I left for college a few years later, she promised to wait on me to come back. Upon my return home, I found out that she had another love.

This hurt me to my heart.

I was considered a gentleman as a student. I was loved by all of the teachers, adored by all of the girls and despised by all of the boys, especially my teammates at the school.

By seventh grade, I was trying out for the first organized basketball, other than midget league baseball, football, and basketball.

I remember practicing all day the day before try-outs, I practice all day and most of the night. That is until my mother made me get my "butt" in the house. I shot at the goal hundreds of times, hardly missing a shot.

See, growing up, we played in the dark because the older boys had first dibs on the court, as well as the field. You can imagine the skills that came out of our neighborhood. I had an outstanding shot for a man of my statue! This surprised many people.

They would often say "Look at this thick strong man with a soft touch."

My whole objective as a big basketball player was to be able to move with the style and grace of a smaller man with a gentle touch.

I took my conditioning very serious even at such a young age. I took pride in the fact that I had always wanted to be the best athlete that I could possibly be. I found great comfort and joy while competing in all sports.

At the try-outs, the coach, Jake Willard, made us shoot the ball fifty times. Charlie and I didn't miss one shot! The Coach would eliminate you if you missed, or looked like you didn't have what it took to be on his team. He was a tough coach!

The coach had cut most of the boys on the team. It got down to two of us and he decided that I shouldn't be on the team.

I remember I begun to cry and complained that I hadn't missed a shot and Charlie backed me up on that , so the coach had me and the other boy, the one who was also to be cut, go to the free throw line and make twenty-five shoots.

The other guy had missed several of his shots during the course of the day as well at the free-throw line.

The coach still felt that I was the one to be cut, mainly because I was from the Evans Hills. We were the outcasts, even though we all resided at the same school and were to play together as a team.

That's when I first experienced the politics that comes along with any sport. As a young person, I couldn't fully understand why I was singled out.

I did make the team and turned out to prove to the coach that I was worthy of being there. I was the leading starter for the team and was the highest scoring player in the whole division.

I scored so many points that the score keeper would pass off my points to the other players.

My best friend, Charlie Baggett was also one of my teammates and was quite a player himself and one of his good friends was the statistician, the person who noted which player scored each point. His name was Julian Brown.

It was said that for every six points that I made, the next six were given to Charlie or James Lee. I guess that's part of the politics that is endured with sports!

I didn't find this out until I had entered college. Some of the guys told me that they did this because they were jealous of me.

I was a good team player even though I endured much ridicule, being an outsider as I was labeled. I was a very humble guy, was and still am.

Never a bragging athlete and having the confidence in myself to be the very best: I had one heck of a seventh grade year!

I recall bringing home my report card and I made a "D" on it. My father really put his foot down and said that I couldn't play basketball.

I was so hurt, especially after all that I had gone through just to make the team. I cried and begged and pleaded. I promised for them to give me one chance to make that "D" into a "B".

I wouldn't stop crying and pleading until finally my mom said that I had to live up to that promise or else, I would get my butt beat and in addition, I would be on punishment for an undetermined amount of time. You can believe that I buckled down and made my promise good.

I wasn't the smartest kid, but I did the very best that I could. Being an athlete, there would always be someone that was willing to do your homework for you. But I never let anyone do mine.

We all try to take a few shortcuts, but I knew that if we got caught, then my father would handle this just as though I had stolen something. I was the kind of guy that was never negative towards anyone.

I wanted to show that I could be as good with the books as I was on the field. I had to work a little harder than most, but I ended up coming out on top anyway.

35

My dad had begun to realize that I, someday, would be a man of my word. This made him very proud.

The same fellows that played basketball also played football at Washington Drive. I played tackle and a linebacker. There were also times when I was allowed to play in the tight end position.

Our football coach's name was Mr. Avant. He taught and drilled the basic fundamentals in me that made me a successful professional ball player. I didn't realize this at the time.

But as I became a professional, I oftentimes think of him and how hard he was on us and how angry I was then. If you made a mistake on the field, they would give you a paddle on the butt.

I can remember once, when I first started playing in the league (school), I didn't get to play in the first few games, so I would roll around in the dirt.

Well, that was in my earlier years and it hurt a lot that I wasn't given the chance to prove myself in the beginning, but I know that things worked out for the best.

Many people in the community were impressed by my basketball skills, but were ten times more impressed once they got the opportunity to see me in action on the football field.

I was mistaken for a brick wall at times by some of the many players who would come in contact with me on the field.

This is how politics are in the sports.

Say for instance William Henry Dobbins's was just as good as me to go pro but because a coach liked me and not William, then William couldn't possibly have the opportunity to prove that he was good, if not better in the pros!

This was a special time in my life. I guess you could say that this was my sprouting years. It's funny how the things that we learn as children can make such a profound affect on us as adults.

The most important things that my parents instilled in me as a young child made me the man that I am today.

Surprisingly enough, my basketball skills were much better than my football skills. As you read through this book, you will soon see that this statement is a strange one.

LOOKING BACK

As a young man, this was a time in history where we would look forward to seeing such singers as: Joe Tex, James Brown and The Mighty Delfonics!

You were a lucky kid if you got tickets to the show. The kids would envy you and try to start some kind of trouble because of jealousy.

There was this girl that I really liked and Ronald McDonald liked her also. He was supposed to be one of the toughest guys in our gang.

That was until he decided that he wanted this same girl and challenged me to a fight in his back yard. I wasn't going to punk out and not show, so I went and took home the glory!

All of the spectators cheered me on in disbelief that I had kicked Ronald's butt. He not only was the toughest, but one of the oldest members of the group.

That day, I, the quiet one, not only won the girl, but I also won a lot of respect from the neighborhood kids.

My very first girlfriend's name was Joyce Getty. This was during my junior high school days. I really liked her a lot.

She was sexy to me, if sexy is a part of a junior high student vocabulary. I recall kissing her on the front steps at her house. We would sit all day long sometimes necking and kissing. That is until one of her parents would come home.

She is now a principal at one of Atlanta, Georgia's more prominent schools.

I carried out the responsibility of watering the plants, taking in the newspapers each morning, as well as the mail each day. I checked and made sure that the doors were locked and saw to it that no one entered the premises. I also fed their dog and cat.

Back then, I found much pleasure in helping to build good athletes from the younger guys in the neighborhood.

It made me proud when they would listen and hang onto every word that I would say. More importantly, my being a pro athlete would make them mimic my style of play or my form of conditioning my body.

My girlfriend, Stephanie McKinney had a younger brother named Quentin. I shared with him many positive thoughts that I had on the physical aspects that one should inquire. This information became influential in making his career successful.

He went on to attend, Appalachian State University located in the mountains of Boone, North Carolina. He was an honor student and an outstanding football player.

Stephanie McKinney's parents had a great deal of respect for me. One summer, her parents gave me the responsibility of taking care of their home while they were going on a trip. They were very pleased with my level of responsibility.

Being a very popular athlete, there was a lot of jealousy from my friends as well as some of my teammates.

Although Charlie Baggett was my best friend, he always wanted to try to take whatever girl I liked and call her, his own. This caused some problem for us back then.

Popularity was one of the prizes for being a good athlete. You could have two or three girlfriends, special privileges at school, such as passes to walk the halls or just whatever a normal student couldn't and shouldn't do, being good at sports gave you.

I say that because good football players' aren't normal people. Extreme measures are always expected from a football player.

When going out with the guys for a beer, we, football players weren't supposed to drink just one beer, they were expected to drink a whole case.

Around the same time that year, my sister told my father that I had taken his pack of Lucky Strikes cigarettes.

My father tore my tail up something awful. I wanted to kick my sisters' butt for lying on me, but I didn't. I took my whipping like a champ.

One day, a famous world champion boxer by the name of Floyd Patterson drove down our street to see one of his family members. All of the kids ran down the street following the car. This was an exciting time for us.

Only on a few occasions did we get the thrills of simply looking at someone of such statue.

None the less, there were a good handful of us who actually made something of our lives, even after the hard times in Evans Hills.

Our little gang would occupy our time by running through the fields and turning flips. We were like gymnasts. We would turn flip after flip, some with no hands others with one hand.

Oftentimes, we would compete to see who could turn the most flips. Yes, I grew up with some very physically challenging young boys who loved sports of all kinds.

As a young kid, I loved reading books. I read books about successful athletes such as Sam Huff, (former player of the New York Giants football team), Chris Hamburger and Dick Butkus, a former player the Chicago Bears.

I always wanted to be called "The Little Dick Butkus". He was a lean, mean, tackling machine. He made you feel that if he didn't like you, then you should look out and get out of his path.

Boy, he was a sight to see! I admired his strength and ability to trample anything that got in his path.

Often we would blame each other for some crime just to get each other in trouble or to cover their behinds from a licking.

My father didn't take to people who would snitch on someone else. Even if we knew whom it was! I often got blamed for many things that I had nothing to do with. I guess this is what most of the youngest siblings endured. But me, I was always the nice guy.

No hard feelings to my sister for telling that lie on me because she might have done me a favor without realizing it. To this day, I never touched a cigarette. Maybe, just maybe, that butt whipping was a good thing after all.

I remember a young man by the name of Melvin Henderson who connected with me when I was around nine or ten years old.

Although he grew up with all of us in our neighborhood, we were not that close, but we had a strange type of connection.

He and I attended the same church and we spent a lot of time there together as we bonded a brotherhood that was quite different from all of the other guys that were in our "little gang". He wasn't part of all of our little devious and mysterious shenanigans. He was different in a good way!

Later Melvin went on to go to Brown University and on to Duke Medical School, located in Durham, North Carolina and became a doctor, an obstetrician, one of the most prominent pediatricians/obstetricians in Fayetteville, North Carolina.

Melvin was scholastically a genius! He was skipped through many different grades, I guess, maybe, that's why he seemed so different from football jocks.

He is one of those kinds of people that you never lose contact with. To this day, we call each other regularly and keep up with what is going on in each other lives. He turned out to be a real friend!

Once I grew up to an adult and found out that he had become an honor student in medical school, I figured it out that our connection was that he too had dreams and aspirations of becoming successful, just as I had!

A WORKING BOY

Everyone in our household had a job as soon as they were old enough to do so. My brothers were much older and began sooner than I.Therefore, I stayed home and lifted weights.

Most people thought that I was crazy and obsessed by training and lifting weights so adamantly. But I didn't think twice about what they thought. I worked, went to school and was a darn good athlete!

I would get odd jobs like cutting grass or raking leaves.

My very first job started out at a tender age. It was at Esquire Barber Shop located on Murchison Road. I was a shoe shine boy.

I remember one week, I was having a hard time making any money and one of the barbers said, "Hey Joe! Why don't you tell them that you'll give them a free shine! This should give you the chance to prove that you can put a shine on a pair of shoes that spit would reflect from!"

I tried his tactic and sure enough, it worked like a charm. I would shine their shoes, just as though they were paying customers. Some of them tipped me and then there were others that paid me in full. I was so proud and amazed that it really worked!

Of course there were those who did take that free shine, but they were the kind of customers that returned each week and paid me what the shine was worth.

I made more money that week than I had ever made. I learned a lot from that and this proved to be of tremendous significance to me, now that I am a man.

It is the little things in life that you might not realize at the time, but these are the things that eventually really matters in your life.

Next door to the barbershop was a restaurant and occasionally, I would go over there to help out in the kitchen by washing the dishes.

My second real job as a young adult was one in which my brother helped me to acquire. It was at a grocery store where he was the butcher and I started out as a bag boy.

My brother and I made sure that our family had food on the table, some of the best choices of meat because we cut it ourselves.

Then I advanced to the produce section and then to the stock/shelf boy. Eventually, my brother taught me how to cut meat in the back.

I finally got a job at Kelly Springfield Tire Factory. There, both my brother and sister worked and eventually, retired from. It was considered a good job to work at the local factory.

The pay was pretty good and it made for a sound foundation for those who would just settle. But me, I had aspirations of becoming successful at something!

Then, unfortunately, I had no clue as to what this might be. I knew however that was football.

In my teenage days, I did many things to earn money. I also tried construction at one point.

Construction is an art within itself. You never think about things such as manholes, do you? Well, did you know that a manhole is sometimes in excess of fifty feet below the ground surface?

This may not seem deep but if you ever had to climb down inside of one then you will know that it takes a hell of a person to do a job of this nature.

I tried it and found that the darkness in the deepest of a manhole is more frightening than the toughest of ninety linemen coming at you full force!

After my supervisor and I realized that climbing down wasn't my cup of tea, they allowed me to be shaken up by being an air-jack hammer man. If you aren't familiar, then it is a machine that breaks up concrete. It was enough to shake and wake up even the dead!

The power and force that is within a jackhammer is amazing!

That same power and force helped me to build stronger muscles than just lifting weights. It gave an account of just why 'Mr. Muscles' was the perfect name.

I thought that if you handled tough things, then they would make you tough. I was correct. This made me tough and helped me to be able to take a good solid punch.

HIGH SCHOOL YEARS

I attended a high school that was almost an hour walk home. Imagine having to walk home after being in school all day and after a hard practice in the game of football.

There were several ways to get to the school, we could walk through the woods, go along the tracks or we could go the long way, around to the highway.

It really depended on how we felt that day which would determine which route we would take. If we thought that we might get a ride, we would often take the route that would lead us to the road.

No matter how tired we were or what the weather might have been, we did what we had to do, and mostly, we enjoyed doing that, to and from!

Seldom did we ever get a ride home, but when we did, Coach Ike Walker would allow us to ride with him in his truck.

Although, there were many different friends that would walk home with us, many days, Roderick Hodges and I would walk home together.

We would stop by our old favorite candy store and get candy and then from there, we would go home to eat dinner with our families and later I would lift my weights. Then it was off to bed in preparation for the next day.

So, it wasn't until I got to my senior year that I began to get rides to and from E. E. Smith Senior High. I guess this was partly because I was one of the star players on the football team.

Anyway, one day it was raining like cats and dogs, so Coach Ike Walker said that he would give me a ride home. I was somewhat reluctant to accept the ride, just out of respect for him as an adult and someone whom I looked up to dearly.

But I took the ride and he took me all the way up to my road and because of the rain, the road was closed off due to the flooding. He tried to insist on trying to get me there, but I insisted on walking the rest of the way.

It has remained in my mind and heart the persistency that he had, just to try to get me home and to keep me from getting wet or sick in that awful rain storm!

That will remain in my thoughts as long as I live. He never knew how much I truly appreciated that ride on that rainy day.

Mr. Miller was our principle and football was his favorite sport. I guess this attributed to all of the big pep rallies that we were allowed to miss our classes to participate in.

It was at Washington Drive that I loved the game of basketball and to me, football was secondary. But once I got to E. E. Smith High School, it spoke for itself that I was destined to play the game of football.

My brothers were into basketball and they were 6"4" or better and I stood only 6"3" and I was considered to be short.

I was stocky built with skinny legs and they teased me about this. This sometimes bothered me. That is until I started playing football and my size made a statement for itself.

I too, played basketball and was known on the court as, "Mr. Muscles", the man with the gentle touch and soft shot. I was very good at the game, but E. E. Smith, was recognized as the school who favored football.

So, I thought that I should go that route and put basketball on hold to try to prove myself on the football field. I not only proved my skills were up to par, but I showed the town that I was versatile. That's exactly what I did too!

My second year in high school, I played starting line backer and offensive tackle. Thank god. I was finally able to prove myself.

Our coaches' names were Mr. D.T. Carter – Head Coach, Mr. William Carver, and Mr. Ike Walker, my mentor. We had one of the best teams around the state.

My sophomore years, I decided to take on a mission of challenging a young man by the name of John Heard. He was the toughest player I had yet to see. Nothing got in his way. He played linebacker as well: known as 'The King of All Linemen!'

One day at practice, the coach asked who wanted to go up against John? There was something in me that made me speak up and say, "I'll do it!" I said it very strongly.

We were then put in the pit. The pit is the front line and you face your opponent face to face, head on. The coach then says, "Hit and you charge and hit one another!"

We would clash like too bull ramming as hard as you can, trying to move that person and pushing and shoving and forcing your legs to drive that person to the ground.

I had a good technique at snapping into the charge position. I would gain my leverage to the point that I would get underneath my opponent so that he had no chance at getting me to hit the ground. That is what I did to get the name of "The King"!

Everybody looked up in awe as they saw me hold my ground and, not being budged! I turned my legs in a way in which John Heard toppled to the ground! It was so exciting!

It was at that moment that the coach, as well as myself, knew that there was another king and that I had a future in football.

You can see in the coach's eyes the amazement and admiration. I'll never forget the gleam in his eyes.

I then earned respect from the team and the community as word got out. That, to me, was my greatest and most exciting challenges in my early career.

This information was placed in the newspapers and from that moment on, many colleges showed big interest in Joe Harris. I got a lot of recognition for being the hard hitter that I was.

I remember playing against one of our cross- town rival teams and my coaches told me to put the wood on anyone that got the football! And boy oh boy, I did just that!

Putting the wood on someone means to place a great, heart-wrenching, solid hit to your opponent.

I had a special way of putting the most ferocious fear into an opposing quarterback and in the linemen that I was up against.

Terry Sanford High School had a running back in this particular game that day and following the advice from my coaches, I put the wood on him.

With the fear that was in my eyes and the force of my punch to the running back when he landed on the ground, made him get up from the field and rush to his coach to say "Tell that quarterback don't make me run the ball anymore. That boy is crazy! I'm not gonna let him hit me again!" I knew then that I was doing quite well as a linebacker!

That running back wasn't the first nor was he the last to proclaim my insanity on that football field!

Shortly after that game, Charlie and I began to prepare ourselves to take the SAT Exam. We studied very hard and were ready when the time came to take it.

Always after each practice, we would have to do sprints, especially after a tough and growling practice. This was thought to push you to the edge of total exertion, which made you stronger the next go around.

Many other times, I recall making interceptions and running them back to score a touchdown.

Dick Walker, Ike's other nephew (Charlie was his nephew as well) would always complain that I would steal his passes.

Dick played defensive back. I would tell him, "Don't just stand there and look at the ball, go out there and get it! Don't let me go all the way!"

One day, my sister asked, "Joe, do you know truly just how good you really are? You have all the people in the neighborhood talking about you like a king and how great you are on the football field. Do you know what it means to be considered the best line backer in the state of North Carolina?"

We once played against Carl Lester Crumpler, the father of a couple of pro football players today and the best running back in the state back then.

We played against his school in a championship game and I hit him so hard in a game, that I knocked him on his back. He was 6'4" and had legs like a gazelle. I, well I'm 6' 2" and 210 lbs, soaking wet!

He later admitted that that was the hardest he had ever been hit. I replied, "It's all about the fight in the dog. If you got a lot of fight in you, you can go along way."

That was one of the old sayings that my older brothers and his friends would often say to one another. I then felt like one of the big dogs!

I ran into him many years later and not so long ago and he quoted that same quote to me as we spoke of the good old times.

During that same conversation, I talked about the wisdom that I had heard and learned from listening to the older guys that lurked through my neighborhood, such as; it's easy to quit and harder to keep going when things get tough on the field. To gain respect from one of the states' fastest and best running backs was a high honor to hold.

Soon after that game, there were several other players on our opposing teams that also admitted being hit the hardest ever by me.

Many of these war stories hit the local newspapers and I soon became the talk of the town!

I used to sit and meditate on how to and not to hit a person on the field and my father would ask what was I thinking.

He would *say* not to be scared, just go out there and "knock the shit out of them." That will slow anybody down!

My dad was a tough man and I always tried to do as he said. So, every time I got a chance, I would knock the shit out of them.

After I was given this advice, many players would say, "Don't give him the ball, that boy is crazy!"

That is the kind of fear that any good line backer should possess! And I had the talent to place fear in mostly all of the players that I went up against!

I look back on my entire career and I remember the times when I would intercept passes and run all the way to make that score.

I also would pick up fumbles to score.

When I made it to the NFL, I reflected on my ways of play during high school and college and I compared the two. They were very much different in comparison, but they were also alike in many ways.

When I entered the professional league, I studied my forms that I used in high school and I went back to that. I was again able to recover fumbles and intercept passes. Exactly how many touchdowns I made during my entire career are unknown at this time?

I dreamed of scoring and hearing the fans cheer me on to victory. These things were part of the goals that I had set long ago. Success!

Success doesn't just happen. You have to set those goals and push to accomplish them. I am very proud that I've stuck to my goals and kept focus on maintaining my spirit and becoming successful.

Our school had a bus in which we called the 'Blue Goose". We traveled everywhere in this bus: track and all other sports and school functions.

Mr. Newkirk was the bus driver and he was proud of the bus. It was quite nice as I think about it. It was blue and gold. Mr. Newkirk made certain that it was clean and shiny.

I can reflect on being the player that stood out the most that year. I attribute this to the books that I had read on Sam Huff, Dick Butkus and Chris Hamburger.

Those books taught me what a true line backer was and what the expectations were for being a good linebacker. This motivated me to strive to be the best.

Each coach had his own way of motivating you. My high school coach would shout out, "Who wants to be in the mighty five?"

The mighty five was the front line and this is where every player has hopes of being. Up front is where you should always strive to be. After that practice and my desire to become the new king, I was on the front line for the rest of my high school years.

All during my high school days, I concentrated both on being a good student and a good athlete. I was Vice President of the student body and focused on those things and not girls.

In the end, I was chosen to be one of a few, High School All American, All East Player, All State and several other honors. That's when all of the hard work paid off.

Unlike most of the other football stars, I was humble and stayed by myself. I felt that by doing these things, they would help me to achieve the goals that I had set for myself.

I loved going to school. Surprisingly enough, I never missed one day of attendance through all of my twelve years going to school. Amazing Huh?

I enjoyed getting up in the morning early and starting my day. I really looked forward to walking there.

Even though it was almost six miles to the school, I enjoyed it tremendously and can recall each day, no matter how cold or hot it might have been!

The pain at a practice made me feel stronger and I really looked forward to that. This made it easy for me to get up and start each day in a positive manner.

I was always one of the first persons at school and was definitely among the last to leave the campus after practice.

I was a hard worker in everything that I did. My father taught this to me. He taught me to believe in God and place Him first and to give every ounce of yourself to whatever I was doing.

Thanks Dad!

Most of the players drank beer and alcohol and would try to "do all of the girls," even if they were your girlfriends! Some even smoked marijuana.

I remember Charlie and the guys would say that it wasn't good not to drink and not to have a girlfriend. I wondered why! But I'm glad that I didn't indulge. I'm thankful that my thoughts were centered.

I went all the way to my senior year of high school before ever taking my first drink of beer and or alcohol. I admit that I even indulged in smoking a little marijuana. I did this just so that I could fit in with the "in-crowd". Bad mistake!

The "in-crowd" consisted of Charlie Baggett, Dick Walker and Floyd Johnson who was my first cousin.

Although, there was the "out-crowd". Those were the guys that did drugs and alcohol on a daily basis.

These were also the persons who, even to this day, are strung out and made little or nothing of their lives... "the out-crowd"!

It wasn't like it was an everyday thing to drink and smoke. We did this on the weekends and when we planned to attend a party or something.

Because I was being an athlete, these forms of extracurricular activities had a negative affect on my performance. I knew this, but I would never say it to the guys for fear of being called a "wuss" or something.

After feeling the affect on my body, I would somewhat try to avoid being put in a setting, that placed me in a position to have to indulge.

Don't get me wrong, the guys didn't, by any means force me to do alcohol and drugs. As I stated, I wanted to fit in.

I had several other friends that played on our football team. Dennis Monroe played safety on the team. He was a good guy.

We became much closer once we grew older in age. He now lives in Atlanta, which is where I reside now. We get together and not only talk of the old memories, but our friendship now allows us to make new memories.

I had another friend in high school. It was Charlie's cousin, Larry Gillis. Larry, and I played on the defense side for the Fighting Bulls.

All through the years that I attended school, there was good old Charlie Baggett, my best friend. He was a quarterback and I blocked for him.

I also played tight end and tackle. In doing this, we had a close bond that laid the ground for an everlasting friendship, even to this day.

Playing tight end, prepared the groundwork for the upcoming year. I won a game playing in that position in my ninth grade year.

The actual play was called a tackle eligible play. That game was played against our good old rival team, J. S. Spivey, Jr. High School.

This is where Charlie, the quarterback throws me, the tight end, the ball and I ran to score the winning touchdown! That was my first of several throughout my career. It was very exciting.

That's when my coach realized that I had an extremely positive affect on our team. Soon after that, I was on the starting line-up.

That year, as a freshman in high school, I was awarded most valuable player in basketball, track and football for the city, I was also captain of the basketball team that year.

I was highly regarded as, Joe Harris, the guy form the low rent district that was so dedicated and had such great hopes and desires.

That year and the next two years, I received five trophies. I was highly honored and recognized. I knew then that all of my hard work was beginning to pay off.

During my sophomore and junior years, our school was awarded Division Champs. In my final season as a senior, we were named State Champions.

We were each highly regarded, garnered many different awards, and broke high school records that had been held by others for years. We did ourselves and our folks proud.

All of this was important to all of us. It helped to build positive attitudes that allowed some of us to propel into professional athletes.

I didn't realize that all of my dedication, devotion and desire to make my dreams come true would take me as far as it did.

I was taught all of the right things by my father back then and didn't realize that those things would have such a significant affect on my life as an adult, but they did... profoundly!

Coach Avant was a tough man! He made sure that we conditioned our bodies before and after practice. And if you had a bad day on the field, he made us run laps around the field. We didn't agree with his style of teaching or his techniques to become a good player.

At the time, we all hated that man for being so hard on us. But looking back and examining what I learned from him, I can now say that I appreciate him and all of his tough and drastic measures.

I was the High School All American Linebacker, All State in Basketball and Football, as well as All State in Track and Field.

In addition to that, I was City and County Player of the Year in basketball and football.

I held a record for being the number one tackler at my high school, leading interceptor as a linebacker and lead scorer as a linebacker. I'm not certain that those records were ever broken.

In high school there were a few football athletes that participated in drug usage. There were many different kinds of drugs, such as marijuana, cocaine, heroin, acid and several different types of pills.

This was partly because of the army base located near the home. This base played a major role in my live and the lives off all of the human beings affiliated, near and around the city.

During my childhood Fayetteville, North Carolina was one of the largest heroin addicted cities, per capita, per size in the United States. There was an army base called Fort Brag in the city and the G. I.'s came in and out of town.

These G. I.'s would smuggle in large duffel bags full of heroin or the drug of their choice. Then there were the ones who smuggled in these drugs not for municipal purposes but their own financial gain.

I always look at my high school years at E. E. Smith High School, as a learning experience, which prepared me for the politics of football and made me comfortable with the football atmosphere.

During my younger years, I didn't fully under-stand what and why politics had such a significant role, not just in football, but all professional sports.

Most importantly, prejudice will arise in ones' career.

Shear jealousy and envy-hearted individuals can make or break a career, be it a professional sport or a high-ranking office official.

That's where the politics come in. At that particular moment, you don't even realize that it's politics.

Politics came into the picture as early as my midget league football days. It did not have an affect on me until I reached junior high and high schools.

I remember the coaches would pick their starting players by popularity or by the neighborhood that you were from: unless you had skills, and I had skills! That was probably the only reason that I was chosen to be part of "The Mighty Five".

Territory has a great impact on the amount of ridicule and politics that might come into play, especially during the years when one is in junior high and high school.

It didn't matter if a person was good enough to be in the starting line up or not. I can recall several teammates that should have been given the chance to prove that their skills were worth showing.

Not just the player's that were blessed to have been "born with a golden spoon in his mouth", as the old saying goes.

One summer, Coach D. T. Carter had a visitor by the name of Bud Carson. He was the head coach for Georgia Tech. I had the distinct honor of meeting him and he made it very clear hat he was interested in Charlie and me.

Charlie and I had wanted to go to the same college, even though we fought over girls a lot. Thank God it was only girls that we argued over. All and all, we were the very best of friends.

I remember attending many different football training camps each summer. They proved to be very helpful throughout my whole career. I placed all the knowledge that I received from each camp, into my skills as a linebacker.

I remember one summer we went to a camp in Greenville, North Carolina. It was a very small town with dirt country roads and a small township area that consisted of only a few two and three story buildings.

But located just inside of the city was a huge college campus called East Carolina University. The college campus was part of the town, which gave the city life.

The camp which I attended that year was headed by a man named Coach Travatran. He was the high school coach in Greenville. He was assisted by Coach Mike McGee and his brother. They were both coaches of East Carolina University.

We stayed in the dormitories and at the end of each day; we looked forward to returning to our dorm room for some well needed rest! Although they exhausted us to the extreme, we still had big fun that summer!

I learned a lot from that one particular camp. I think that I got so much out of it because it had a wide variety of different sessions. We had a session that taught us weight lifting, basketball, and group exercising.

There were also classes on the fundamentals for each type of player that makes up a football team - running back, wide receiver, linebacker, tackle, etc

I broke a record during the camp in weight lifting that summer. On an incline, I pushed 565 pounds with my legs! For a high school player, that was almost unheard of especially with the skinny legs that I had and my body weight size which was 215 pounds. I had very strong upper body strength and was quick as a cheetah! I proved then that I was very strong and could hang with the best of them!

An all-pro football player by the name of Sonny Randall, who played wide receiver for The Saint Louis Cardinals, gave us the incentive to give our all at the camp.

He was one of the best wide receivers to ever play in the N. F. L., and to even get the chance of being on the same field with him, I felt was a great honor. He asked, "Who wants to go against me?" When he asked that, I stood up and took on the challenge.

I always had the will power to take on different challenges. It didn't matter to me how big a person might be, or how great he might have been.

I felt that taking on a challenge gave me the sense to measure myself to a certain degree. If I didn't come out on top, then that meant that I needed work in that particular area.

But as history goes, I don't recall ever losing a challenge.

It was at that moment that I paved my way towards the direction of stardom.

So, I played one on one with Sonny Randall and he couldn't believe the moves that I made on him. I would make a move and he was so astounded and shocked by it that he asked me to do it over and over.

I was on him like "white on rice" each time. He was amazed at how far ahead I was at covering him. The coaches were impressed too!

I showed skills that I had wanted to flaunt but had yet to find a challenge that was challenging enough to make a difference. Based on my skills and abilities, that day, I proved who I was and that I was ready for even more challenging experiences.

I earned respect from him and many others that had attended the camp that summer. In addition, the students that I went to school with were envious of me because, I took home yet another record. I even smirked in their faces.

But as I said before, I was very humble and didn't brag about the incident. I was still very proud of myself.

At that particular camp, I did an awesome job at learning and understanding all of the technical aspects that were taught and was named Student Camp Attendee of the Year!

It was then that Coach McGee tried to recruit me to come to East Carolina University. But I was only a sophomore and still had a couple of years left in high school. That was the first college that somewhat showed interest in me.

That sophomore year was great for me and it was the beginning of my making a name for myself throughout the state and eventually, throughout the United States and other parts of the world!

Charlie and I would decide whose house we would eat at, his or mine. All of the parents of my teammates enjoyed feeding us and of course, we loved eating, being growing boys and all.

Charlie had an aunt named Ziff who could cook the world's best homemade biscuits! She would always make certain that we had some biscuits to eat everyday! She took great care of us. We loved her very much.

My mom and Charlie's mom would take turns cooking after practice special dinners for us. Sometimes it would be for the whole team! They were the greatest, so caring and loving.

It was very special to me that I had such a good friend like Charlie. It gave me the opportunity to see first hand some of the things that was in his life.

He was not from Evans Hills. He was from a better section of town where the people were a little better off than I. Not that that made them better people, it just meant that they were able to see and do more than what my parents could afford.

I was taught to treat everybody the same. I have lived by this all of my life, regardless of what situation a person might be in.

For instance, his family took summer trips that I would dream of taking. The most that my siblings and I would do was to go to my grandparent's farm to spend each summer. And then, we had to work.

Although I still enjoyed that immensely, it made for a "heck" of a way to spend our days off from school!

The difference in our lifestyles had no affect on our relationship. Still, Charlie and I shared everything!

Overall, I would say that throughout my days growing up in Fayetteville, North Carolina, was a positive influence.

My four years in high school was a lot of fun and very stimulating to my mind. To be one of the top athletes to come out of E. E. Smith High School was a reward within itself. But the knowledge that I acquired was even more productive.

Values made me a person with a reputation that I'm proud of. Thanks Mom and Dad!

EVANS HILLS

I came from an area called Evans Hills. This place was consumed with muddy, winding roads. It was a town that was filled with loving people.

People that taught us value, such as honesty, respect and discipline. It was considered somewhat of a place where poor and under privileged families would reside.

All and all, we might have been poor, but we had food, although we often went to school without having breakfast. Most importantly, we had great parents.

I would sometimes wonder why there were some students at our school who would spend most of their time in the cafeteria. They would bully others and take their food.

I found out later that they didn't get enough food at home so they had to steal food in order to make it through each day.

A lot of the athletes were from broken homes, from the drug-infested section of town and they were hungry most of the time.

So how do you think this affected the boys once they got to the football field? The coaches were extremely hard on these boys because they lacked stamina and energy.

You never know how well off you are, even though you may think things are bad until you see and hear the problems of the next person.

There were a lot of talented people who came from the small town of Fayetteville, North Carolina.

Several things that stand out: the tree that I used to climb as a child and that path that we traveled on our journey from place to place or house to house. Everyone knew and looked out for each other, kind of like one great big large family.

If you did something wrong at a friend's house then that friend's mom or dad could and would discipline you, and then go and tell your parents what they did. The persons' parents would say, "good, you should have whipped his butt."

I can recall going swimming naked in a creek filled with water moccasins and a snake-infested creek called Snakey Beach. It was there that I first learned to swim. I loved to pass my time away by swimming. To this day, I swim an estimated 40 laps per day!

When I go to visit Fayetteville, I still drive by that same tree that I used to climb as a kid and remember all of the good times. A place that was safe, secure and inviting and a place I call home.

There was a guy named Daniel Virgil and he had gone swimming with us one day. He jumped off the ledge into the muddy creek and cut himself.

When I say "himself"", I really do mean "himself ". Unfortunately, this cut ended up causing him to loose one of his testicles. This made all of us think twice about running and jumping off of that ledge!

I guess by the town being so small and maybe because there wasn't a whole lot for us to do, a person found one of their specialties and concentrated solely on perfecting and mastering that skill which they enjoyed.

A lot of professionals were reared from that little place on the map. There was a lot of talent to arise throughout history, in the small town of Fayetteville, North Carolina.

Just to name a few, Doug Wilkerson. He played offensive guard for the San Diego Chargers.

Dee Hardison was a spectacular defensive tackle for the New York Giants.

There was Charles Waddell who left Southern Pines, NC to play with the San Diego Chargers.

A wonderful sportsman, whose name of Bob Macadoo played professional basketball.

I'm certain that there were many others who went into the profession of sports. Even though they are not mentioned by name, they still have my respect.

During my school days, there were a lot of smart kids. There were kids who studied hard and looked at things outside of the things that we saw on a day to day basis.

Some of us just looked and then there were the few of us who actually had the drive and ability to step outside into a world of professionalism.

It was rough in the little town that we called home. Just down the street from our house, was a shotgun house where at least once a years, there was someone stabbed to death.

Then, of course the casual gun shots that accompanied the area. It was tough.

Up the road, however, from our house was peace. A place where kids grew up doing all of the normal things that kids did.

Everyday our mothers and fathers worked hard and tried to do all of the right things, living as though we were in another place and time.

Next to Evans Hills, was a section of town called "Cape Fear Courts". It was one of the roughest areas known through out North Carolina.

This area was made up of people that weren't doing so well and were having a hard time. "Plain and simply, just down on their luck". I guess their anger made them hostile and mad at the world.

Therefore violence played a major role in their daily life schedule.

But then there was an area called Broadell Drive. This was the area in which the high school was located and also the area that the people who were somewhat well off lived, such as my friend Charlie.

It has always been my opinion that wherever a person is from, will determine what different opportunities might be available to him or her. That's how politics fall into play as far as geography is concern.

MY PARENTS

My mother was my true strength during my preparation into adulthood and professional life as an athlete.

She was the one who stood by me when my father would try to take me away from what I enjoyed the most: football.

My dad was somewhat of a violent person, especially when he was drinking. He was an extremely strict father who demanded that you do as you were told. He was mean and stern in his own beliefs.

It was mom who was there for me when I would cry if my dad would punish me by not letting me play the sport. She was the one who told me to not let go of what I believed in.

She whispered many nights that my father *was* only one of the small obstacles that I would face on my long journey to stardom.

I don't think that it was apparent to my father just how good I truly was as an athlete or how devoted I was at the game until some of the gentlemen in the neighborhood strongly brought it to his attention.

It wasn't until then that he even came to one of my games. When he finally did see me play, he then tried, in his own little way, to show some form of support.

I had an injury, I hurt my ankle pretty bad and my father watched me put ice on it all day and night. He knew then, exactly how dedicated I was at striving to be the best that I could be.

He watched how good I was even though I was hurt. I was in a lot of pain, but that still couldn't stop me from playing in the game.

I think that that was when it started to "sink in his head" that I would never give up playing football.

Eventually he got the message and gave in to the fact that nothing, not even him could stand in the way of what I believed in. Finally, I got the respect that I had wanted from him.

My mom died at the tender Age of forty-six years old. It was a tough pill to swallow, but I found peace once I realized that she was taken to a much better place.

The sentimental words that she spoke will be with me until I die. The special moments that we shared as a family will reign in glory. I love you mom. You'll forever be in my memory.

Before she passed away, she told me "to go forth with my dreams and aspirations and that she had faith that I would be blessed with whatever I set my mind to do". It was these words that made me more determined to be as successful as I could.

Unfortunately, she died before being able to see me play in the United States, but did get the pleasure of knowing that I had made it to the professional league. She told me to go and play the game like I had never played before.

It's because of the love that my mother so desperately bestowed upon me that this book is even possible. For this, to her, I dedicate my book: Thank you Mom!

(Dad)

All of my life, I feared my father because of his violent temper. He was a good man, but mean!

I would watch him hit my mom and it made a sore spot deep inside of my heart. I still loved him but it was a kind of love that is hard to describe.

Watching him hit and slap my mom hurt a lot. It hurt in ways that is indescribable. And for the life of me, I don't know why she put up with it for all of those years.

I had nothing but the utmost respect for him. After all, he was our dad, the breadwinner of our household and the man that my mother loved dearly. She put up with him for reasons unknown to my siblings and me.

Yes, sure we had some good times as a family, but I always knew to stay out of his way and everything was going to be alright.

He gave me a lot of wisdom. I guess this is why I am the man that I am today. For that, thanks Dad.

It took some time for him to fully understand the seriousness that I had when it came to football. But once he saw me play that one time, he became more aware.

Of course, I didn't gain his support until long after he realized that I was determined to succeed at reaching the goals that I had set for myself.

My dad was extremely strict on us kids. It made all of us angry, but it did pay off. My mother and father reared us in a way to do all of the right things.

I guess I got being such a hard and dedicated worker from my father. He was respected as the breadwinner in the house, although we all brought in income.

The death of my father was a bitter one. When he died, he was about the age of sixty- eight and died in a very strange manner.

He was driving down the road one day with a very young lady, a lady almost my age, when his misfortune came about. You can let your imagination take you where it may lead, smile.

I loved my dad then and I will love him when we meet again in Heaven.

My parents taught me to be very respectful of adults and individuals. This one thing made me become a better man. I can appreciate this now.

BEING RECRUITED

During my senior year in high school, there were several different well-known colleges that attempted to recruit me.

There was Wake Forest, Duke, North Carolina, North Carolina State, Georgia Tech, Michigan State, Vanderbilt, Tennessee, East Carolina, Utah, Wyoming, Kansas, and Élon College in North Carolina.

A&T in Greensboro, Shaw, North Carolina Central, and Tulane University in New Orleans, Winston Salem State and Fayetteville State were also attempting to recruit me.

I guess you say that is a mouthful, huh? And quite impressive if I might add!

Although impressive in numbers, I already had a dream to become a leader at a major university. And to gain the recognition that I had planned for myself it required that I attend a white college.

Naturally, taking and passing the SAT was going to be the key to entering a white school.

I was blessed to have scored high on the SAT. This gave me a lot of freedom and the opportunity to go to any school in the country. This score came from a lot of hard work and long hours of studying.

I suggest that each and every person that has set high standards for themselves realize that a high SAT score is the tool that is needed to open the doors to the college campus of your dreams... hard work and dedication.

During this recruiting stage of my career, each college wanted to give me a big party; they fed me all of the big steaks at some of the name brand restaurants and allowed the key athletes to take me out on the town in each of their cities.

Of course, it was exciting to get such recognition from all of the top schools but I ended up choosing Georgia Institute of Technology in Atlanta, Ga.

Once, I was down at University of Wake Forest being recruited and Kenny Garrett, also from Fayetteville, North Carolina, was taking us around the city of Winston Salem,

North Carolina. Kenny had some type of Vodka and we got drunk that night!

Dexter Pride and I were wild at the party that night. We were acting up and wrestling as though we were already past college and on to being pro-football players. We were actually tackling one another right there in the middle of the party and having a good time.

Dexter was a running back and I was a linebacker and we would ram each other and say, "Here we go, here I go" to the top of our lungs. That saying was the highlight of our storytelling the next day.

Everyone was trying to get us to stop horsing around, but we were totally out of control, and that's when we both began to throw-up those wonderful steaks that felt so well going down. Only they didn't feel so good coming back up.

I was so drunk that they had to place me in the back of the car because I couldn't get any fresh air. I tried to breathe, so they let the windows down and went back inside the club. They left me breathless and continued on their mission to party and catch girls!

I was sick as a dog the next morning. One of the worst hangovers that I ever experienced! Also that hangover was the first of many during my lifetime, but it stands vividly in my mind!

If I knew then what effect alcohol would play on my life later in the years, I never, in a million years would have ever touched that stuff.

While I was being recruited at University of North Carolina, I overheard the coach and some of their players talking about Charlie Baggett and me.

I recall hearing him say, "If we can get Charlie, then we will get Joe!"

They knew that we were best friends, but what they didn't know was that we were smart and to put us to the challenge turned us both off. It placed a void in our minds that they were toying with us and took us for granted.

I was no sucker! And I was going to prove to them that it wasn't wise for me to overhear them say that!

This made me determined not to choose that school, but Charlie ended up going to University of North Carolina for the first two years of his career, but transferred to Michigan State where he graduated. But I felt that it just wasn't the college for me.

Anyway, during our stay there, we had Ike Oglesby, running back, showing us around and we, of course went out to eat. I don't remember the name of the place that we ate at, but I remember having the biggest steak that I had ever seen!

It completely covered a serving platter! And to this day, I have seen some big ones, but never one that big!

At this college, Ike tried to hook us up with some girls so that we could get the real taste of what being in college was like. From what I understood the girls on campus at the University of North Carolina really put out, if you know what I mean!

Georgia Institute of Technology was only given a quota of recruiting one black football player per year so, Charlie and I went there to be recruited. And, Eddie MaShan, first black quarterback in the south and Greg Horn, the first black running back at Tech, were taking us around and showing us a good time.

I must say, we did really have a great time while we were there!

Eddie and Gregg had put together a little party for us at The Royal Coach Hotel. Back then, it was a "big time place" especially being in Atlanta.

They rented several rooms there, got us some booze and called up my old girlfriend from high school, Stephanie McKinney and many of their girlfriends. We had one great big party that night. It is one that I'll never forget!

89

We partied so long that the girls that went to Spellman got in trouble because they missed their curfew that night.

The girls didn't mind being in trouble because Charlie and I were only in town for that weekend and we were going to fly back to Fayetteville on that Sunday and they wouldn't get to see us for a long time afterwards.

Therefore, I guess you could say that they took their punishment in stride!

My girlfriend went to Spellman College also located in Atlanta. Actually, the college campuses were somewhat neighbors in location.

Everybody used to say that because of Stephanie, that's why I chose Georgia Institute of Technology. But that wasn't true; I had made it up in my mind during my junior year at high school that I would go to Georgia Institute of Technology, solely because of Bud Carson.

He was a very close friend of my high school coach and when he spoke at our senior banquet, I was completely sold on attending Georgia Institute of Technology.

While at Georgia Institute of Technology it rained and I remember watching the game on television and I kept close watch on how the players were able to play on that muddy grass field! The football field was subsequently changed over to astro-turf.

The first piece of astro-turf that I ever saw was a sample sent to me by Vanderbilt University. They were trying to recruit me and thought that the opportunity to get to play on such material might just win me over, wrong!

This amazed me. All of that Georgia red clay!

I recall them announcing on the loud speaker that some of us had come all the way to see 'a rainy night in Georgia!'

We found this to be amusing because of the old Ray Charles song, "Rainy Night in Georgia".

I was allowed the privilege of meeting a lot of top athletes around the country. Athletes such as: Marcus Mooney, a running back for West Virginia. He was from Shelby, North Carolina.

There was Robert Pullium who played defensive tackle for Tennessee. Charles Waddell was a running back for Carolina. Dexter Pride from Southern Pines went to play for Minnesota.

Roderick Hodges went to North Carolina Central. He lived right down the street from me when I was growing up.

There were a lot of parties, lots of good food, many girls and lot of fast times. The traveling and getting the chance to meet a lot of the top college athletes in the United States was grand, but I am proud to have chosen Georgia Institute of Technology.

There are various qualifications that a player must attain if he or she wants to be recruited to a top school.

First and foremost, having good grades is one of the most important qualifications that he or she most maintain. Keeping your grades up throughout junior high and high school is crucial. The grades that you make then may not seem important at the time, but they will remain as a reflector for your entire life.

Being a sound citizen is also a plus. There is no college in the world that wants to recruit a player that has a bad reputation to represent their team.

Not only is it important to your possibilities of being recruited into college, but it plays an important role if, say for instance you have hopes and dreams of becoming a politician some day. Good citizenship will prove to be the most extreme factor in your life, while you are growing up!

In hopefully becoming a college recruit, one most attain valuable skills in his or her field. Such as mastering the strong stance of a linebacker or having perfect technique as a good tennis player with a good back swing.

Having great physical condition not only is a plus while being in the line for a college to recruit you, but this will play a major role in the coming years. This can and will protect you from injuries.

If you have the love and desire to adore a certain sport, this will aid you when it comes down to respecting the game that you master.

I feel that if you have all of these qualities and am certain that you are ready for the college life and have dreams about your future, and then I would say that you are a prime candidate for being recruited to any college of your dreams!

OFF TO UNIVERSITY

The very first time I experienced an airplane ride was when Georgia Institute of Technology flew me to Atlanta. I was kind of afraid but I knew that it would be one of many plane rides that would be a big part of my future, especially with the dreams that had I for myself.

Charlie Baggett, Marcus Mooney, Charlie Waddell and I were the four recruits that were allowed the opportunity to visit. We were all extremely excited to fly!

Once we got to Atlanta we were escorted by Eddie McShan and Greg Horn. They were the top players of the Georgia Institute of Technology Yellow Jackets at the time.

They took us around the town and showed us the campus. They introduced us to a lot of people and boy oh boy, were we ever excited!

As I mentioned earlier in the book, Eddie McShan was the first black quarterback in the south. He was a very neat dresser and an outstanding individual to say the least. I had admired him from afar even before I had the chance to be chaperoned by him.

Greg Horn was the first black running back at Georgia Institute of Technology and they called him "Touché Away"! I would always ask him for food and he would always make sure that I had enough; boy did I love to eat! I did then and I still do now! This was another outstanding young man whom I'll never forget.

I guess you could say that we were proud to be the guests of such an outstanding university. We received a lot of attention from the coaches and professors. For if we choose to be alumni.... then we were their future!

Of course my girlfriend from E. E. Smith High School, Stephanie McKinney was in Atlanta attending Spellman College, located not too far from. Georgia Institute of Technology. This ultimately made my trip more than worth the wait!

It gave us the opportunity to see each other and make up for some lost time, if you know what I mean, smile!

Once we got to the university we partied hard and then it came time for business! Were we destined to be a part of the Georgia Institute of Technology family?

Georgia Institute of Technology was a university that didn't have but a couple of black athletes. And I felt that it would be a great place to put down some roots.

There were only a total of twenty-five African Americans that attended at the time that I was there! If I recall, there were only a total of five black females.

But if you were to go there today, it looks like one of the top black college campuses. I guess you can say that the first blacks at Georgia Institute of Technology opened up a lot of doors for African Americans!

I really like the campus itself. I adored the place where we dined and eat our meals! For the football team our meals were free and I especially liked that part.

But overall, the campus was lovely! It was landscaped to the fullest and the dorm rooms were clean and spacious.

Being the big guy that I was, I needed lots of space and I also wanted a college that offered plenty of good food! After finding all of this out, I knew that Georgia Institute of Technology was the place for me.

In addition to being a great admirer of Budd Carson, the head coach and my high school coach, D. T. Carter's were best friends. I decided that I wanted to be a part of this wonderful institution!

Bud Carson graduated from the University of North Carolina .He then moved on to become the head coach at Georgia Institute of Technology

I used to watch Georgia Institute of Technology on television and I thought that they were a good team. They had lots of small players who were very quick on their feet. This drew my attention and I knew that they could use a big and tall guy like me.

My size and the size of their players gave me hope that I could make the overall picture complete for the team. I knew that I had a lot to offer their organization!

I would study their plays and watch their formation in awe!

There were many reasons why I wanted to attend. Georgia Institute of Technology not only because of the good free food, or the wonderful football teams and their records, but I wanted to be the first black defensive linebacker to play on the team! I was not only the first linebacker, but, the very first black defensive player.

That was another one of the goals that I had set for myself once I began to contemplate which college that I wanted to attend.

The year was 1971 and to be one of the first blacks on the team, they expected a lot of you. They expected more from the blacks than they did from the other players. You can say that we had a lot to prove to them.

But being as determined, as I was, I wasn't gonna let them think that I wasn't up for the challenge!

In the beginning, it was kept sort of hush, hush that I was black. People didn't know that Georgia Institute of Technology had their first black defensive linebacker, me.

Under the helmets, it was hard to tell if a player was black or white. I wasn't dark, I was a light individual.

Not that it would have been a problem, but I guess in 1971, it was not too acceptable by the community. But it was the day and age when blacks were being introduced to the white colleges all around the country.

Needless to say, they gradually introduced me as yet another black affiliate of the Georgia Institute of Technology football team.

I was truly accepted and admired by the fans once I showed that I was more than up to par to play for the team. I proved that I was an outstanding football player as well as an upstanding pillar of the community.

To this day, there is yet to be a black person to reside in the management offices at Georgia Institute of Technology. I'm not just speaking of the athletic department; I'm talking about the entire administrative team for the school.

This bothers me even today! We need to have some Black people on their administrative team so that we can have our say and make some of the concrete decisions for our people. At least there are more blacks that have been allowed to study there!

There are 75% black players for the Yellow Jackets and all white administrators. I feel that a change is long over due!

I learned right away that life wasn't fair. Fair in the sense that there were only three blacks on the team. For instance, when we went out to eat, and the majority of the white players wanted steak, but we wanted chicken: we were definitely out numbered. Whatever they wanted went!

"There again, politics fell into play!"

I felt that I was being discriminated against and I simply went along with the program. Once a few of the white guys got to know me as a person and not just a statistic, they often asked me why I played along with the system.

I expressed that "it was my time to make a place on a team that would eventually advance me into the National Football League Association!" I told them that "I was destined to be a professional football player and that if it took being belittled then that was what I would endure!"

I would then ask the white guys why they choose Georgia Institute of Technology? They would say that their daddies made them come. They said that their fathers had graduated from Georgia Institute of Technology and that they wanted to keep the tradition!

I would think that my answer to them placed a few things on their minds. Maybe after my answer to them, it instilled a bit more positive influence for them to take their careers more seriously than to just pacify their fathers.

I believe this to be true because shortly after that conversation, and after our four years at college, there were several players who became professional athletes.

To name a few: Billy Shields went off to play for the San Diego Chargers. Randy Rhino went to play for the Montreal Alouttes, and Steve Raybell started playing for Seattle Seahawks. I'm certain that there were others but they are not forgotten.

The white boys on the team were given the opportunity to play for the distinctive Georgia Institute of Technology team because their fathers and fore fathers prepared a path for them to follow.

The black players, however had no past heritage at Georgia Institute of Technology therefore they had to make a name for themselves, and to prove that they were worthy of being a part of such a prestigious institution!

The classes were not the norm. They were extremely hard for a person like me who had a problem with retaining all of the information.

When I was a junior, I was pretty well known throughout the campus and well liked by blacks and whites as well.

Also, the fraternities were well connected with the professors. I was told by Bo Bruce, on the day before an exam to just put my name on the test and that I would get a call later that night to find out what score I wanted to make on the test.

I said, "What?"

I found out then that the fraternities on the hill had a copy of every exam at the school!

Since I was well liked by all, they decided that they would hook me up.

I didn't agree with this because I was taught at a very young age to work hard and to not take *short* cuts.

Therefore, I never cheated on any tests throughout my days in school and I certainly wasn't going to start then.

Hell, I had already made it to my junior year, why mess up now?

But as you well know, temptation is a mother! So, I did as I was told. I put my name on the test and walked out of class.

That evening, I was called and they said, "Hey Joe, what do you want to make on the test?"

I couldn't believe it!

They said, "Just meet us over at the frat house."

When I got there, one of the guys in the fraternity was a grader for that particular class and I was given an "A" on that exam!

I realized then how these guys who partied all of the time were on the Dean's List without studying at all. They had connections and they stuck together.

There were many of them who graduated Suma Cum Laude. That means with great honors!

That was the easy way out of a tough situation, especially, when you had been up partying all night the night before and didn't study. Actually, only when I had no time to study did I use the fraternity graders and his expertise.

It always stood out in the back of my mind those stern words that my father had said to me many years before. I knew that my dad would never find out, but I was scared!

I was scared that my dad might find out and I would never live it down.

Not that he would or even could beat my butt like he did before, but I felt that it would be a disgrace to him if I was caught.

Also, that was one way to get black balled if it should ever arise!

POLITICS! And the white boys had all of the control!

There are many different situations that arouse for a white institution to pick up a black football player. There are the income standards of the player, as well as the scholastically requirements to maintain a certain grade point average.

There are the community values that a play must have in order to possess the standards that a significant and outstanding player must maintain.

Imagine coming from an environment where a student has nothing but his family and barely the necessities that life requires. As compared to the white guys who had everything at their "beck and call": all the way down to a path or pattern that their fathers and there fore fathers laid for them!

Again, politics! Politics not involving gender, but race!

I endured all of the challenges that the 1970's had to throw at me! I fulfilled all of my dreams and aspirations! Thank you Jesus!

I remember this one game, I took a cut because my knees were hurt and the coach knew it. I should have been off somewhere soaking my knees or putting ice on them but the coach had other things in mind for me.

He made me play in the game and I ended up tearing the cartilage in my knee from the wear and tear of the game.

I was pissed and in a lot of unnecessary pain, which could have been avoided had my coach put the color of my skin aside and done the right thing by letting me sit out that game.

Remember earlier in this book, I discussed politics? Well this is a fine example of the kind of politics that accompanies athletics.

The day that I hurt my knee at practice, my new girlfriend Mary Beard was at that practice. I had often told her not to ever come to watch my practices because if I became cut or something, it would be troublesome to me, not to mention, embarrassing!

I knew that my knees were getting weak and I just felt that it would not be a good day for me on the field and sure enough, my knees gave out on me. But the coach still insisted that I play in the next game! I was so upset!

This was something that was gonna happen anyway because I had signs that my knees were weakening, but I was still upset!

Even though I was hurt and injured, I still had one hell of a game that day. I made a couple of outstanding plays that is sure to be in the record books!

The big time colleges are making millions on the successes that a young college student's puts forth and the only thing that the students receive is an education!

Not that that couldn't be a priceless item, but during your college years, you struggle and put forth all of your abilities to become a good football player while the college itself makes millions off of your talents! This is what happens during a talented black athlete's experience.

POLITICS!

I know many people who attended black colleges like Morehouse University or even a school that is not made up of all black students such as, U.S.C., University of Southern California, and they say once a Trojan, always a Trojan. This means that they will take care of their own!

The players on the West Coast did not have to endure a lot of the racial criticism and ridicule that we as blacks here in the south had to endure.

U.S.C. tends to look after its people long after they have graduated from the school.

I feel that this is an area that Georgia Institute of Technology needs to focus on. The university should give its students and players more incentive to study hard and it will probably help to boost up the amount of enrolled students at the school!

This is one of the downfalls that I experienced. But I didn't know this at the time that I choose Georgia Institute of Technology as the University of my Dream.

Georgia Institute of Technology is very weak in this area.

We as black players stuck together, but Georgia Institute of Technology as an institution was not in unity with its players or even the students for that matter!

There were many great black athletes that attended while I had the honor of going there. Let's see, there were Greg Horn, Eddie McShan,Eddie Ivory, David Sims, Ruby Allen,Lucius Sanford, Cleo Johnson, Peewee Barnes , and Don Bessillieu.

This was before anybody knew that there were any blacks that attended. Remember, we were covered, by our helmets on the football field.

We were the ones that started the "fight" at Georgia Institute of Technology! We were the one's that got the ball rolling for all of the athletes of today.

Georgia Institute of Technology is in need of some black, administrative people on its staff. Sure, there are some white people that do their job and they do it to the fullest, but how can a white administrator know the needs of a young black student from the hood?

Overall, my four years in college were good ones. I wouldn't trade the experiences for the world! My experiences help to make me the man that I am today!

It was hard, especially coming from a family that only had the necessities of life. I mean the cleaning of ones clothes for instance. The laundry bill alone would make or break a student that wasn't as well off as the next one!

I will not lie, it was difficult for me coming from the small lower middle class family in which I evolved, but all of life's challenges paid off in the end. I succeeded at my goals.

I endured the obstacles that were standing in my way. I went "without" lots of times and I made it through!

Being part of the football team, I never really went hungry, but I did do without many of the luxuries that a student from a more prominent family might have had. This only made me stronger in many aspects.

I always felt that there must be a way to make Black players feel comfortable with the environment in which they are suddenly brought into.

After all, they are making millions off of the player and his or her talent and capabilities!

I have often heard that a black college or university looks after the Stars that tend to play a major role in their school, such as a number one player that rolls in the fans and makes the school money.

The white institutions, however don't invest in the comforts that a person that brings in mega millions should have or be given!

Coming from E. E. Smith High School in Evans Hills, North Carolina and entering into a world that society has labeled as a white prestigious university environment, you would think that being the star that I was, my life would have or should have been much easier than it was. But I tell, you, I went through a lot just to make it through!

It was somewhat of a culture shock. I had to pretend that I understood things the way that they were, when in actuality, not understanding it in the least bit. This was considered growth to me: to be able to fool society into thinking that you do belong in this white man's world!

I think that the system is designed to place blacks into a "cultural shock". When we endure these things that are placed in our paths to try to stop us at succeeding, that's when you know that you truly do belong in this society!

It wasn't easy! It was hard to be exact, hard *as* hell! But I toughed it out because I had goals and dreams and I was determined not to let anything stand in the way of my success!

I would say that this is only my opinion, but I lived through the atrocities of going to college in a day and time that was unlike the times of today!

I lived through being pushed out of the lime light because I was a black football player, simply because society wasn't quite ready for another black face to take the glory of stardom!

I must say that I am proud to have set a path for the brothers of today so that they won't have to go through the struggles that I had to go through as a young black athlete in a white man's world!

The average regular student SAT score is 1200, whereas, an athletes score is only *850* on the SAT. This is a large gap in numbers when were talking about scholastics!

There are so many leaps and bounds in this aspect alone! There are different situations and challenges that a normal financially deprived or blessed student had to go through.

More than just finances, going from the hood of North Carolina to a 99% all white college had a great affects on me. The tone and dialect of a person always needed to be improved upon!

I remember this one guy named Bo Bruce; he always wanted to help me out socially. He always wanted me to go with him to the Kentucky Derby each year.

I often felt that this was to groom me in the social settings of life, which it did! And each year, we had a great time there!

The Kentucky Derby was quite a different culture for a black man and I was game to pick it up!

He talked me into going to see Led Zeppelin at the Atlanta Fulton County Stadium! This was a white male rock band. This quite naturally expanded my spectrum on the ways in which the white boys partied.

These things in the long run made a difference in the lifestyle that one becomes accustomed too.

This is only one of the different cultures that I was blessed to have the chance to experience. Picking up on the different verbal dialects can, will and did change me as a person.

Being exposed to the different cultures and dialects of the different places in the United States, made someone who didn't know me wonder, is this guy black of white when speaking to me?

It wasn't just the tone and dialect of my speaking, but it was also the fact that I was *no dummy!*

I kept a grade point average throughout my four years in college around a *C+* average. This was almost unheard of being a jock. Football players are labeled somewhat similar to a *dumb blonde*, so to speak.

But I was taught at an early age that grades from the very beginning would play an important role throughout my entire life. This encouraged me to always study hard and keep focus on my goals!

So naturally, I spoke intelligence that made other wonder, "Who is this big guy?"

Mom And Dad

My Son

My Wife and I

Me and the Family

Me sacking yet another quarter-back

To: Joe
Friend Always!
Wendell Tyler #26

Wendell Tyler Rookie Year

MORE ABOUT GEORGIA INSTITUTE OF TECHNOLOGY

To me, Georgia Institute of Technology was a great institution to get a good education. Getting a good education gave us all something to fall back on when and if our talents on the football field gave way.

The professors that taught at Georgia Institute of Technology were some of the best in the country.

My favorite professor throughout my four years at Georgia Institute of Technology was Professor Long. He was one of my biggest fans, a football fanatic! Maybe that's why we clicked and hit it off so well.

The scholastic challenges were phenomenal! It was a hard school when it came down to the books! I struggled many nights studying and praying to pass that exam on the next day!

I can remember sleeping at the library on numerous occasions just to make the grade. Oftentimes, going without a meal because I knew that if I were to get up from my studies that I wouldn't return to study anymore.

Therefore, I did without because I was determined to study just so that I could still play on that field. And to play on the field gave me a confident feeling that I would be that much closer to my ultimate goal in life, the N.F.L.!

It wasn't just studying, but to retain all of the information that you covered was a job within itself. That really was the hardest part of it all!

To find out twenty years later that I was dyslexic made me understand why I had to study extra hard.

To be able to keep a 2.6 grade point average at a place like Georgia Institute of Technology was an awesome accomplishment.

To be able to play on this football team you need to keep a 2.0 average. I was one of the blessed ones.

My most profound and outstanding achievements while I was at Georgia Institute of Technology was, that I became the very first black football captain for the Georgia Tech Yellow Jackets team!

Impressive? Well, I earned it plus, a whole, hell of a lot more!

Leadership ability was another goal of mine. I possessed it and did a darn good job of passing on positive thinking to some of the guys!

I have always felt that if the system was to do whatever they needed to get what they expected out of a player then we as players should do the same thing, get all that we can out of the system!

That's why if you are given the opportunity to get a good education: make the most of it and get all that you can get! That's what I did, I got all of the education that I could but the establishment gave so little back to me!

Once we played against Florida State University and I will never forget that one of their players stated, "I see yall have a nigger boy on the team!"

He started laughing while one of my teammates named Bo Bruce said, "What did he say to you Joe?"

I said, "Don't worry about it Bruce, I got this!"

That very next play of the game, I will never forget that the one that called me a "nigger" broke through the line and I knocked the "holy hell" out of him and he lay there on his back with the wind knocked out of him!

I stood over him and said, "That's that nigger boy style!" You remember that when they take you off the field!"

Everybody laughed and cheered, "Way to go Joe!"

I had a lot of help during my college years. Maxie Bond, my linebacker coach taught me an awful lot during those four years. I am grateful to have had the opportunity to study under him.

He was a professional linebacker in his time and eventually came on as the linebacker coach. He helped to make me take my talents to the next level.

Georgia Institute of Technology was known for having some of the best linebackers in the country and I was proud to be one of them.

I felt that I was needed while on the team. They depended on me to make that big play and to stop the opposing linemen and I must say that I did a job, well done!

This would naturally put a heavy load on one's shoulder, especially a young man from the hood, but this is something that I wanted, I wanted to be the very best of the best!

I had always sought out to be needed and on the team I felt needed!

One other thing that I learned from attending the Tech was knowing the difference and understanding which differences makes winners or losers.

Winners win with class! They have a classy way of life. They put God first and families next. They try to do all of the right things in life. These are qualities that make up winners.

Plus, never forget where you come from and never disrespect anyone!

Losers on the other hand, lose with no style or finesse! They lose without pride or dignity which instills negative forces in their lives. But when one loses with the pride and dignity of a "good sport", they too are considered winners!

It took me learning from the best of the best how to be a good loser and they taught me how to become a great winner!

This is one of the most important things that I learned while attending Georgia Institute of Technology!

Going to Georgia Institute of Technology wasn't always fair, but I had made it up in my mind many years before that I was going to be someone someday and the situations helped me to make that dream come alive.

It was hard to maintain that "C+" grade point average and it was even harder to keep up the image on that football field. But determination and lots of hard work kept me going.

I eventually was inducted into the Georgia Institute of Technology Hall of Fame! I, to this day hold records that have yet to be broken after all of these years! That, my friends is what hard work and determination can and will award you.

You must stay strong and focused at all times, no matter what circumstances and obstacles may come your way!

During the time that I played, I played three years on the main team and one year on the freshman team.

I was good enough at what I did as a linebacker that I was the number one tackler for each season and to this day, I still hold this record!

Looking at this record today, makes me proud because no one has been able to even come close to breaking that record.

No one has come close to becoming the "Jolting Joe". The man to put that forceful hit on someone. I was quick on my feet and even though I was a linebacker, I still scored several touchdowns throughout my years at Tech!

With these qualities and being the gentleman that I was landed me more opportunities than the average player might have had.

I must say that I was truly blessed to have the physical abilities that I was born with. I was blessed to have the courage to strive for the goals that I had set for myself. More importantly, to be successful.

Time flew by and my career exploded into something that I, at the time didn't truly know how to grasp!

I mean, I know that I knew what it was that I had worked for all of my life, but, at the time, was I really aware of what was happening?

It all happened so suddenly. Although, four years isn't really sudden but when you are on a tail wind of great play, hard hits, and good grades and living the life of "Riley", I have to ask myself, "What happened?"

I'm not complaining by any means, but it makes one wander, where does time go?

Live each and every day as though it is your last! Put all that you have into whatever it is that you set out to do. Make the best of everything that you place your hands on, or make the very best at whatever it is that you are blessed to be a part.

During college, again I say, it was tough! I remember one time, my car, which was a tan colored Volkswagen Bug had a little glitch and needed fixing. So, I went to the head office and I told them that my car was on the fritz and they told me to just take if to the Volkswagen Dealership and get it fixed!

It is the little things in life that really count. Even if it is only a couple hundred bucks. This really meant a lot to me because I was poor!

Coming form a poor family from a small town, my mom and dad would send me whatever they had to spare. Twenty-five or thirty dollars wasn't a lot but back then, one was grateful to receive even that! I know that I was.

On the weekend, the dining room was closed and we needed that extra cash to get food! Yes, I was grateful for any little bit of money that came my way.

My older brother and sister would send me five; maybe ten dollars to try to help out my mom and my thanks go out to them, even to this day!

The Varsity, a restaurant known for its wonderful hamburgers was one of the places that we spent a lot of time at on the weekends!

Occasionally, I will go by there just to get one of their naked steaks or one of their naked dogs. That was simply a hamburger or a hot dog! Those were a couple of my favorites!

I was lucky to have had the skills to be fortunate enough to be accommodated by the Georgia Institute of Technology Athletic Association.

Again, that's what great skills, hard work and a lot of determination will do for you!

There were a lot of successful people who attended Tech. I remember this one young man by the name of Mackel Harris. He played linebacker and one of the fastest linebackers that I have ever known. He was a 9.4 sprinter, very quick on his feet!

Although Mackel was fast and quick and a great tackler. But, he never broke any of my records such as being the number one tackler. He was good though, but just not quite good enough.

Mackel Harris was a late draft pick for the Denver Broncos but after being drafted, he didn't make the cut.

He went on to work for Life College in Marietta, Georgia and later went on to be the number one recruiter for a Chiropractic College located in South Carolina.

I did keep up with Mackel. We were once quite close as friends, but as time moved on, we drifted. Mackel was one hell of a guy. I give him much respect!

At the end of one Spring season, James Kelley, a genius, Greg Horn, Rudy Allen and I were hanging out in front of the dormitory and James came out of the building and ran up to me and said, "Hey Joe, I want you to try something with me!"

I said "What is it?"

He says, "I would never give you anything that would hurt you, now would I?"

He handed me this little, tiny piece of tablet, similar to a small dot on a piece of paper.

I placed it on my tongue and swallowed. For a few minutes I asked, "What is it going to do to me?"

They replied, "Just wait and you'll find out!"

We were all talking and I began to feel the effects of the drug known as acid!

I remember laughing at everything that was spoken and they questioned me by saying, "What are you laughing at Joe?"

I said, "The hell if I know!" and I continued to chuckle with laughter. The guys were not laughing with me but more so at me.

That day, we walked the entire downtown section of Atlanta, all the way to Piedmont Park and back to the Georgia Tech campus.

I can vividly remember watching the sun reflect off of the leaves on the dogwood trees with total amazement!

One of the dorms had glass front and a glass back panel simulating the door. I went up to the second floor and they yelled, "Don't let him near that glass window!"

I can vividly remember it seemed like going through a mirror room at the local city fair!

I remember thinking how close the ground looked and it seemed as though I could just reach out and touch it!

They jerked me back from the edge and said "let's just take a walk". That's when we walked through the entire city. Laughing and talking. We made it a point to find everything about the policeman on the corner extremely funny. Although he found little humor in it!

I said shortly ago, that James Kelley was a genius. I say that because he was the only guy that I've ever known to be able to smoke a joint of marijuana, play loud music, drink a beer, study and make an "A" on a differential equation exam! Electrical engineer he turned out to be. I wonder where he is now?

During my reign at Georgia Institute of Technology, I had a narrow window in which to view the big picture. I was the first black linebacker and therefore, I always felt that I had something to prove to them.

They expected a lot out of me. They expected me to make a lot of the major plays. If there were more black players on the team then I would have felt that I had a little more support from them.

But when there are only three or four players that may have come from the same small town in the hood as I did, I'm sure that they too were feeling that they had something to prove as well.

We supported each other at best that we could and we survived it all! Praise God!

We were out numbered to say the least, but as the season rolled on and after the first two years, the white players eventually treated us as though we were all one big happy family.

In the beginning, there were those few that may have had a problem with showering with us black players, but as I think back on it, it wasn't prejudice on their part; it was a feeling that was bestowed upon them from their fathers and fore fathers. They weren't to blame.

Georgia Tech had a maintenance crew, which consisted of all blacks with the exception of the managerial team. These were people that we black student tended to converse with, simply because they too were blacks!

Those were the very few other black people that we had the chance to see. But if we had enough spare change and could spare the time to go off campus, maybe on the weekends, then we naturally saw a whole lot more.

Those were the blacks that lived and grew up in Atlanta.

Again I say, we paved a path for our young brothers today! I am quite proud to have been able to contribute to our society as a whole!

There was a situation that arose when Georgia Tech had the great opportunity to play in the Liberty Bowl and Eddie McShan was not allowed to play in that game.

It was the final game of the year and he had taken us to that point. We all felt that it was unfair that after getting us to that championship bowl game against the Georgia Bulldogs, the coach allowed for a white quarterback to shine and reign in the glory that Eddie had brought our team.

All of the black players on the team were told by the coach that if we participated in the boycotts then we would lose our scholarships.

We won the game and each and every player that played in that game wore black bands around our jerseys in honor of Eddie and the unfair way in which he was treated.

Politics! Racial politics made it very unfair for Eddie and we were all hurt and upset by this!

Many political black leaders came down and gotten involved because they too were upset about this. They tried to get the rest of the young black players to not play in the bowl game for the simple reason that it was racially unfair for Eddie!

There were boycotts, demonstrations and many pickets behind what had happened to Eddie.

Some of you may remember all of the media coverage back then. As I said before, we paved the way for our young black men today!

I stated a bit earlier in this chapter how other teams tend to look after its players. For instance, U.C.L.A was a team in which Wendell Tyler played for and he was given the opportunity, along with all of the other players on that team to be the star, so to speak! An outstanding player!

Look at Southern Cal; it produced great players such as O.J. Simpson! He built it up for Marcus Allen, Anthony Davis and Charles White to name only a few!

Take note: these were all Heisman Trophy winners!

But teams like that really tried to give each and every player the opportunity to shine in their own glory and to make something of themselves. They backed their players long after they were finished with their four years of college, unlike Georgia Institute of Technology!

I just felt that I should voice what I felt about the many different situations that differ from college to college.

I must also reiterate on the fact that the players on a football team go out onto the field and they take extremely dangerous chances at being injured. This is all for the establishment in which they are a part of.

They take these chances of becoming injured all for a team or institution that cares little for them in the end! Indirectly speaking: Georgia Institute of Technology!

The players are the ones that bring in the fans and the fans are what make the establishment earn money, millions of dollars. And the players, namely black players get so little respect from that organization.

It is totally ludicrous!

Georgia Institute of Technology did not have another defensive linebacker on their team until my senior year in college. His name was Lucius Sanford. He was then and will always be a good friend of mine.

I remember being so excited when I found out that there would be another black defensive linebacker for our team. I felt that because there were two black players playing in my position, we would have more power when it came down to some of the decision making... not!

I did all that I could to build him up emotionally by sharing words of wisdom and encouragement. We became the best of friends and we still are today.

Lucius Sanford turned out to be one of Georgia Tech's three time All American players while he resided at Tech.

He was an exceptional player and he went on to play for the Buffalo Bills in New York. He was lucky enough to be one of the great ones that were drafted in 1978.

Lucius was one of the tacklers that everyone tried to avoid!

I tried very hard to explain the political stand point of being one of the few selected black players for the team. In time he grew to understand the nature in which I was explaining.

The West Coast didn't have as much racial tension as we did here in the South, and I was hoping that he had come from the west coast, but he came from right here in the city of Atlanta from a school called West Fulton High. But old Lucius eventually understood the politics of the game!

Lucius wasn't really used to being around white people, especially since he came from a predominantly all black high school.

Yes, it was a culture shock to him as well, but he soon learned what true politics and racial tension was all about!

Lucius went around campus not speaking much and staying pretty much to his self! Until he got to know me a little and since I was a senior, I pretty much knew my way around and I knew the do's and don'ts so I took him under my wing!

Today, Lucius works for Georgia Tech in the athletic department. He is not, as of now a part of the administrative heads, but keeps up the good work Lucius, I know that you will be one of the first black top administrators at Georgia Institute of Technology someday!

Yes, Lucius works in the athletic department and yes, they do have one black head coach on the basketball team, but there is somewhat of void there if you ask me!

During the entire four years that I was at Georgia Tech, there were only about twelve black players that played for the Yellow Jackets in the whole four years while I was there!

And up until my senior year, there were only the three of us, Greg Horn, Eddie McShan and myself. So my senior year, the Yellow Jackets exploded with color by adding an additional nine players!

That is a very low number when, if we look at the statistics of the number of blacks that make up the team today, it is substantially greater in numbers as far as the number of black players!

I only say this to give you an idea of how it was back then to be the only black defensive player for such an outstanding institute!

BASKETBALL

The Yellow Jackets basketball team wasn't a team that blacks could play on, we had a team that was called the G.T. Triple A's. This was the team in which all of the black students had to play on.

And there weren't any fraternities but we were given a house, just a place where we could hang out with ourselves: "us blacks". It was called "The Black House".

Our basketball team was very successful! I was the leading scorer and captain of the team as well.

We were allowed to play for the Yellow Jackets before the real team came out onto the court and also during halftime of their game.

I remember sitting in the stands while the real game was going on and I recall hearing some of the fans say that they enjoyed watching the black team play and that they especially got fulfillment out of watching Joe Harris play.

They said that they would like to see me play more! They said that if they had me then maybe their team might be doing a better job, that they might even win that game!

That really made me feel special. Special in a sense that I still had a good shot from when I played in high school. Little did they know that I was the leading scorer even back then!

Basketball was a good sport for a football player to play in order to help to maintain his condition. Maybe that is one of the reasons that I enjoyed playing the sport, it helped to keep my reflexes in tune!

To guard a point guard or a shooting guard on the basketball court is very similar to the way in which a lineman would guard a running back.

It was extremely exciting for us when we won the intramural game championship game against the faculty,

The 'Black House' wasn't a house like the ones that the real fraternities and sororities had. It was a house that was located just off the campus and was one of those houses that we might call a fixer upper. It wasn't real run down, but I had seen nicer in my days, even back then!

It had about three bedrooms and a very small bathroom that had green tile formed along the walls. Shabby carpet the color of dirty sand and believe me, it was dirty!

We spent many nights in that old house recuperating from a hangover or staying there because the party never ended from the night before!

Now the white fraternities and sororities had nice three and four-bedroom house with ceramic tile laid floors and carpet of its natural color!

But we never complained once. We had our place and we knew that. And as long as we didn't overstep our boundaries, then we knew that we would have little or no trouble!

But back then, that was Georgia Institute of Technology way of life!

We had a program when I first came on board, where they separated the team and did what they called a positive motivational course. I was on the side of the team that had to set goals for us and then we would meditate and write it down on paper.

I felt that this was an exceptional thing that we had to do and it really helped me a lot.

If I were a teacher today, I would certainly add this exercise to my daily routine.

I'm not really sure who made up this exercise, but my hat goes off to them! Because of the way in which it helped me to reach some of the goals that I had always had, but hadn't quite reached them and at that point in my life, wasn't sure which direction I needed to go in order to reach them. Thanks... whoever you are!

In 1974, I graduated from Georgia Institute of Technology with a business major. That was one of the proudest moments of my life.

But the time that I was more proud of myself was the day in which I was drafted in the seventh round, by the Chicago Bears. This was the same year that "Walter 'Sweetness' Payton was drafted in the first round!

I felt as though I had finally succeeded at what I had set out to do all of my years! From grammar school, to junior high and all the way to high school.

Then in college, my talents were taken to the extreme level and I showed the world that I was N.F.L. material.

Keep in mind that out of all of the players that make up a team, there are only two, three, and seldom, four players that will be looked upon to head to the National Football League. I was one of the fortunate. But then as you go on to a pro team, you are suddenly faced with the reality that everybody is just as good or better! If you can accept that and still maintain your status as a great player then, absolutely, you are pro material. But, only if this is what you have strived for fought for and prayed for all of your life as I had, will you succeed at taking it to the next level. Or, shall I say succeed at putting yourself in the position to possibly be taken to the next level.

THE DRAFT

Just before graduation from Georgia Institute of Technology, one quarter before the end of my senior year, I was amongst 100 fellows who had the possibility to be drafted.

If a college gets four players to become part of the draft then that school did great for any particular year. Most colleges are profoundly lucky to get one or two players that might get drafted into the National Football League.

Not that the luck falls on the school, but the luck and blessings are placed on the draftee. The school just adds another notch into its belt. It gives them a chance to say, hey, in 2004 we had four draftees or three draftees. That is just an example.

When the scouts are looking for their draftees, they are very demanding and arrogant. They want to know if you have the capability to be at their beck and call at any given time. They want to see you hunger to be an N.F.L. player.

They will come to your school and at any given time, ask you to do something out of the normal.

You can be sitting in class and they will come to get you out of class to, say for instance, and run the 40- yard dash. Right in the middle of final exams! This is around the beginning of April each year. The draft usually falls at the end of April.

What really bothers me is the fact that all year long, the scouts have watched all of the college players at the games and on films and they wait until the time that you are most vulnerable, exam time, and they come and they judge you.

A player didn't know back then if he or she were on the possible list of being drafted, it was the luck of the draw, so to speak.

You didn't know if you were going to be drafted but the coach knew.

Now, they have Pro Day set aside for all college campuses. This is a day when all scouts come to visit your college and take an overall look at a particular player.

But when I was in college, they just showed up on campus and interrupted your whole day! But then, that was a good thing!

Now, they also have a program called a Combine. Each player is taken to Indianapolis and is tested, mentally and physically to see if they are N.F.L. material. If they pass all of the tests that are given by the N.F.L. then and only then are you eligible to become a professional player.

It doesn't seem fair that the N.F.L. can watch you play all year long on tapes and at the games and then when it comes down to Pro Day and The Combine, they judge you for your performance throughout your career.

You cannot measure ones standards just from one or two days being with them in the flesh and face to face.

If a particular player is having a bad day on Pro Day and during The Combine, then, they are passed right on over!

It is an extremely stressful period for all players who are possibly nominated as a draftee.

This is when a player gets the chance to see the real deal of what makes up the National Football League!

Just think, if you are a 40-yard dash runner and you are a linebacker, if your average run is 4.5, then you're quick! But say for example on Pro Day, you are sluggish and aren't really up to your best, then the N.F.L. has to option to say, "Oh, he isn't the type of material that we need on our team!"

You are judged from one simple performance, even though you have performed well the entire season or four years in college.

This will affect many young men and the dreams that they have dreamt all of their lives! Just one bad day and they could lose their dream just that quick, one performance.

Look at all of the years of hard work and agony that a player must endure to attain the status of possibly becoming a pro football player.

You could be the one player that ran *25* touchdowns in on season and still judged from one performance.

I feel that it is highly unfair to be judge in this manner. I feel personally that there should be different rules and regulations that a scout should be forced to follow.

POLITICS!

But this is their way of gaining total control over a person. Their ultimate goal is for a player to be at their total disposal.

But times have changed since the time when I was drafted. My son had to endure many night of stress because of the way in which they do the drafts now.

Many days before the draft, I had hoped and prayed that I would be drafted that year.

On the day of the draft, I was chilling with my girlfriend, Mary Beard at her apartment, just relaxing. I didn't watch the draft on television that year because I was so wound up and geared up on the thought that my entire future depended on the outcome of that day's draft.

The day that I had longed for and promised my mom that I would become a pro player, all rested on the final outcome of that day!

The next day, I went to school and one of my coaches said that the National Football League had called wanting a phone number where I would be on the day of the draft. I told him that I was at my girlfriend's house.

That was one of the most exciting days of my life! Coach Ken Blair told me that I had gotten a call from the Chicago Bears and that I was drafted in the 7th round! Back then, there were 17 rounds. But today, there are 7 rounds.

(See many jobs have been cut since 1974- *75)*

With total explosion, I shouted and jumped with joy! I wanted to see this day all of my life. But more importantly, I prayed that my mother would live to see me be in a true professional football uniform!

Don't get me wrong, just to be drafted, doesn't mean that you are a professional football player yet. There are still many trials and tests that a person must endure before being eligible to walk out on the field for a professional team!

Back then, there were 17 rounds in the draft and when I found out that I was drafted in the seventh round, I didn't feel too bad with the numbers. Plus the fact that I was drafted with one of the most outstanding athletes of all time, Walter "Sweetness" Payton. I was honored to be eligible to be on the same team with him. He is now in the National Football League Hall of Fame, along with many other wonderful legends!

Once you are drafted, you still have to make the cut. After it is decided that you have made the team, then it comes down to negotiating your contract and this will result in receiving possibly a signing bonus.

At the time when I was drafted, the signing bonus was merely $6,500.00. But today the average signing bonus is $350,000.00. That is an example for a 7th round pick. But if you are good enough to become one of the first or second-round picks today, the signing bonus is far into the millions of dollars!

When negotiating a contract, it is good to have an agent. But back when I was drafted, it really wasn't enough money to have an agent.

Just because a person lands a contract after he or she has been drafted, doesn't mean that they are set in stone. There is still a long road ahead in order that you might hold onto that position with that team.

There is the great possibility that if a player doesn't play in the first six games then that player is subject to not getting the things that were promised in the contract that was signed by all participating parties.

Let's say that a player does make it to the sixth game and after that, he doesn't play anymore. Then that player is only eligible to receive half of what was stated in his contract

But not all contracts are the same. Each contract differs from one to the next. And depending on each contract will determine if a player can and will be subject to getting cut at, during any time during the first few games in his contract career.

Yes, a contract is merely a legal agreement in which the N.F.L. makes in order to cover them, not the players!

Please, if you have made it to the point of negotiating a contract with the National Football League then please, please, invest in an attorney so that he or she may review your contract and all of the fine print that it entails.

And simply pray to Our Father in Heaven that you succeed in finishing out a season without injury!

If a player is injured in the first or second game of the season then depending on their contract will decide if they are eligible for any of the funds that are placed in his or her contract. The National Football League has the option to tear up a given contract at any time!

All and all, keep a look out for your own back when signing or negotiating a contract.

That basically sums up what a draft really is about. Of course there are more technical aspects of becoming a draftee for the National Football League.

But, I'm certain that if you have made it to that point in your career, then you are sure to find out that all that is presented to you may not be all that good for you.

I remember the day that I found out that I had been drafted very vividly! I was so happy. So happy by the fact that my mother who was somewhat ill at the time was able to see me succeed at my dream of becoming a National Football League player.

I was so happy when the coach told me that Chicago had called me.

When I returned the call, it was explained that they wanted to discuss my future with whoever was handling it. I told them that my coach, Maxie Baughn and I would supply them with all of the necessary information.

I didn't feel that I needed an agent, although I had a few that were contracted, so Coach Baughn and I negotiated the final contract.

They explained that this phone call was just a welcoming call to inform me that I had been elected as one of the lucky players to have been drafted by the Chicago bears.

They went on to tell me that I was to fly up to Lake Forest, Illinois for a small mini- introductory camp hosted by the Bears.

I couldn't wait to get there. I counted each passing moment with shear anticipation!

Everyone around me who were almost as excited as I was. But then again, there were those few whom were jealous, simply because of the fact that I had become one of the people that went down into the history books by having my name placed as one of America's *1974-75* National Football League Draft!

My jersey number with the Chicago Bears was *"50"*. I was so proud to wear that jersey. I was always number 50, 51, and 52 and once in Canada, I was number 45. They said that I was so quick on my feet that I fit into the running back series of numbers.

I have to give honor to God that I was able to sustain the contract that I signed in the beginning and live to play in more than just the six-game spread, but I was blessed enough to play for over ten years with the N.F.L. even though I was back and forth, from the Canadian League to

the National Football League. They were still all
professional leagues.

THE NFL

Being a part of the National Football League is a situation, not a luxury! It is a profound system to be in and to have had the honor of being a part of. However, what is good to you may not be good for you in the long run.

I want you to stay with me on this one, because it may become somewhat confusing to some of you and it may be self-explanatory to others.

I would like to start this chapter off by telling you a few of the stories that I experienced while I was in the National football League.

But first, I would like to explain that these are my experiences and they should not in any way have any reflection on the others who have been or are a part of the Nation Football League.

These are my thoughts, opinions and experiences.

When a football player goes through the transition of playing college ball to playing pro, there are many different situations and emotions that come into play.

First of all, during tryouts, in the very beginning, a player is blessed to experience the feeling of playing with the best football players in the world and with that comes, mixed emotions.

Some of those emotions are: am I good enough? Can I be the person that I'm expected to be? Will I be one of the many that will go through the misfortune of being cut from the team? Can I make an impact on the veteran football players that had made up that team in the years before me?

Will the players and coaches like me as a person in general?(Asking this makes you realize that you are up against a spot in the industry that has been filled by another player who has possibly been on the team or in the league itself for many, many years. Saying that, one must face the fact that they are expendable and that there can only so many stars. Keep in mind that it is all about politics.)

Will I be able to manage my salary to the best of my ability in a way that will be in the best interest of my family and me? Do I have all of the necessary team players in my personal life to help me stay focused and to aid in guiding me towards making the right investments throughout my professional football career? And will that career be as promising financially beyond the realms that my contract states in the distant future?

Will I end up failing as a man by turning to drugs and alcohol like the media leads us to believe? (The media searches and seeks for professional athletes when they fall down. And they feed on things of that nature to capitalize on a top story.)

Can I survive the season without injury? Will I be able to withstand the physical trauma that I'm about to embark upon? Can I live up to the expectation of the fans that support our team? Also, will they be gentle on my name as a whole as they go through their own personal emotions if I make a bad play?

Is the National Football League all that it is cracked up to be by the media and society as a whole?

I can answer the last question with a big NO! The media and society leads us to believe that the National Football League is full of glamour and riches but that is very far from the truth to say the least!

The league only pays the big bucks to a select hand full of players that tend to make up the majority of plays that it takes to win a game.

These are the players that make the headlines and bring in the revenue to pay the salaries of the players on the team, the coaches and the people that make up the entire N.F.L corporate force.

To sum it all up, a player goes through some major emotional trauma, much like the physical trauma that he or she has endured through their high school and college years, which is the same trauma that has brought them to this point in their career.

After I was drafted and I made all of the necessary cuts in order to officially be considered as one of the Chicago Bears, I was elated with joy!

Elated with joy that "out-shined the sun in the sky!" I had worked hard enough to fulfill my dreams and all of its requirements and now, I am still alive to tell about my story and the story of what the National Football League is really all about!

Again, I must express the fact that these are my opinions, thoughts and experiences and they should in no way reflect others who have been a part of or are presently affiliated with the National Football League.

After signing my contract, I played with the Chicago Bears for only part of one seasonal year.

Once a professional football player reaches the point of retirement they often times tend to need additional ways of supporting themselves.

After all, the amount that an N.F.L. retired player's pension isn't as glamorous as it was when he was a star or owned and earned the title of a professional football player.

Again, the media only tells society half of the story and most of it is untrue. Maybe I shouldn't say untrue but miss leading might be a better choice of words. This is where having a good education comes into play.

When an athlete is first exploited into the industry, they will almost play in the league almost for free. They start off by giving the athlete a little bit of an income to make the player feel as though playing for the N.F.L. is a grand gesture or a top-notch position. I will not say that it wasn't good at times, but by retirement time, it all seems so small.

In the beginning of their career, they are so elated with being a professional football player that they tend to overlook the fine details of their career and when they reach retirement, they have so little to fall back on.

Example, a professional basketball player's pension plan is a lot different from that of a professional football player's.

They are allowed a percentage rate increase depending on the cost of living towards their plan. But the N.F.L. has none of that. The N.F.L.'s pension is just what it was at the beginning of the original contract.

A man by the name of Gene Upshaw, who is the National Football League's Union Supervisor. His job is to keep things afloat for those of us who made it to the retirement stage in the professional world of football.

At present time, Gene Upshaw currently is the one who is helping to keep the football retirement fund available.

Gene Upshaw is a retired veteran for the Oakland Raiders and played the position of offensive lineman.

Specifically, Mr. Upshaw is working for the active players and not the retired players. He is working hard for the current players and the ones that make the league what it is today, not the ones that worked hard and are forgotten

Maybe not so much forgotten, but, they have been tossed to the side. Tossed into the archives like molded bread tossed into the wastebasket.

Once a player has reached the point of retirement, it is totally out of their hands as far as negotiating their settlement. It is widely up to Mr. Upshaw and I must admit he has ruffled a few feathers since taking over the leadership role of running the Union.

After discussing our current situation with several of the other retired veterans of the N. F. L. there is much conflict and many complaints about the way that the operation is being run by Mr. Upshaw.

See, Mr. Upshaw was given a multi-million-dollar salary, a Lear jet and many other amenities for taking on the task of Union Leader. This being said, just whom do you think that he is really working for? My answer is himself, the owners and the current players in the National Football League.

As the league has improved over the years, one would think that they would take a little consideration for those who made the National Football League what it is today.

I think that it would be too much like the "right thing to do!"

The National Football League is one of the top corporate associations in the United States and they average hundreds of millions of dollars each year from players such as me who worked really hard for the titles and the positions that we played.

They should be willing and very capable of sharing the wealth. Only it is a thing about, "what have you done for us lately". In other words, they tend to have forgotten who made the N.F.L. as successful as they are today.

The year that I was drafted, a coach by the name of Jack Pardee out of the United States Football League, the

Birmingham Stallions, had just landed the position of head coach for the Chicago Bears.

He was a special friend of mine. I was honored and happy to become a Chicago Bear and with him leading the team, I was sure that we were out to win the Super Bowl that year. But as you well know, a player may or may not stay with the team of his choice. It is the luck of the draw when it comes down to the N. F. L.

A linebacker by the name of Eddie Sheeks and I had the opportunity to work out together and to study the defensive linebacker strategies during the summer after college.

Eddie was a good friend of Jack Pardee and so I kind of had the inside scoop. He was aware of the defense that Jack liked and he and I took it to heart. I was a rookie and had the distinct pleasure to work out and learn plays from a professional football player during that summer, made me stand out above the rest.

Jack Pardee was the coach of a World League team located in Alabama.He was selected as the head coach of the Chicago Bears. Both Eddie and I were selected to play for the Chicago Bears and go with the new coach.

Eddie had tremendous skills as a linebacker.

Again, I guess politics came into play because although I was a great football player and there were many others like me, it is who you know and not always what you know that can get you ahead of the game. You can be the best guy and not even make it. So don't be discouraged just stay in school and get educated.

I'll never forget it, Eddie had a Lincoln Continental and he had a tarp that he covered the car with that read "Fast Eddie" painted on it.

Eddie lived in the east portion of Atlanta, near Murphy High School, and it seemed that he and I were a sure thing. I was so elated to spend that summer working along side of a wonderful player like "Fast Eddie".

Eddie and I would go the college athletic department and we would work out doing squats, pull downs, bench presses and lots of a jogging. We would do five-mile runs on a golf course that had lots of hills. This helped our endurance and stamina to reach new heights.

Mostly we did our workout with the weights. I recall learning a tremendous amount of skills which stuck with me all of the days of my life.

Eddie was very familiar with the ways of Jack Pardee and what he was all about. So Eddie and I focused on all of the things that would make Jack notice us. This prepared me for the practices that would eventually make me stand out like a sore thumb. I gained extreme recognition from Jack as a coach.

Those days really had a profound effect on my memories that started me out in my football career. And it was great players like those guys that made a significant influence on my determination to become one of the players that would go down in history and having my name a household item. Thanks guys!

To Be Blackballed

Being blackballed means to be cast in to the *sea,* so to speak with no way to get ashore. It means that you are placed on a list that is somewhere out there and if your name is on it, you are, just what is say, black balled!

To be black balled means that if during one's career, he or she does something that is out of bounds or against the rules of an establishment then you are put on the list. If you are in college and placed on the list, then no professional team will touch you, or if you have gone pro then no other team will want you.

This includes a college establishment or professional team or one of its components.

Let's just say for example that you are in college and you do something to get into trouble with the law, or you do something that causes an embarrassment to the institution such as drug or anything, you could very well be placed on the black ball list!

Now if you already play for a specific N.F.L. team and you do something to cause shame upon that team of the

N.F.L. then there again, you will be black balled.

My best advice to high school students is to keep your nose clean! Stay out of trouble. Practicing these measures will start you on the right track so that once you enter college; you will have studied and learned from the previous players who were black balled for various reasons. This will enable you to not follow into their footsteps and stay on the right path.

Starting out early doing the right things not only applies to athletes, but it applies to all aspects of life.

Common sense is human nature! Each and every one of us knows what is right and what is wrong.

Stay clear of those negative forces and practice being a good judge of character. Simply, know the people that you hang around.

You may not do anything directly, but, suppose you are with a couple of guys and they just happen to decide to rob a bank or hold up a store, there goes your reputation, freedom and career!

Sometimes, we must weed out our garden so that our flowers can bloom, think about that!

It may sound as if being placed on a simple list might not stop you from succeeding if you are an outstanding player.

But, what I say, "to be put on a black ball list can and certainly be the end of one's career!"

I said earlier in this chapter that no one will touch you; if no team will touch you then it simply states this, you will not be picked up by any team: college or professional.

No establishment wants a negative person representing them by any means!

No matter if you are the best player ever, if you are placed on this list then you have failed! Only under extreme circumstances will a pro team think twice about picking you up.

To have a good reputation means everything, but to have a bad reputation means more... you are a nothing, a nobody.

Throughout my career, during college and pro, I have seen many football greats fall to the sideline because they had done something to shame an establishment. To name a few, there was the great Hollywood Henderson. He played for the Dallas Cowboys. He was blackballed because of wildness and drugs.

Then there was me, Joseph Harris, playing for the LA Rams. I didn't have the position as starter even though I made big plays. It was because I was only a 7 round pick and not a number 1 draft pick. This meant that I was used when they needed plays because I was a big play maker .The public and the newspapers ask the coaches why I wasn't always the starter.

The number 1 draft picks were not doing what I was doing on the field. I also did not make the million dollar contract of the number 1 draft picks even though I was the best linebacker.

To explain it a little clearer, the N.F.L. invests a lot of time, money and effort in choosing their draft picks and I was a seventh rounder. To be better than one of their first round picks caused them to have public problems such as: embarrassment and questions about what they were doing.

Many questions can and will be brought on by the fans when they look at things like that. Therefore, the N.F.L. finds any excuse to make themselves seem right.

Fair, the N.F.L. isn't! But hey, that politics! And politics is what the N.F.L. is mostly made of!

I am not saying that if a person messes up with the system that there is no coming back! I'm only saying that it is a hard challenge to regain a reputation and it is even harder for a team to have faith in you that you will not shame or embarrass their establishment again.

Avoid any unnecessary chances. Avoid any and all people who might place you in bad situations. That is the best advice that I can give you.

I am not prejudice or anything, but we as black people need to stick together and share good advice!

We just need somebody to stay behind us and *give* us a little backing to help keep us focused. It is very easy to fall and become victims of certain circumstances.

The N.F.L. can help to put us in these negative situations as well. Read and reread the chapter called, "Are You Ready to Be a Pro" and you will see that some of our young black brothers are placed in difficult situation where they tend to fall. They fall because of the N.F.L.!

MY ADVICE TO DREAMERS

When I become a professional football player, I got the privilege of being backup to the Great Chris Hamburger! He played for the Washington Red Skins.

I remember thinking how proud I was just to be on the same field as him. That's a heck of a thing to one day meet some of the same people whom I idolized as a child.

Many kids could only dream the dreams, but I was fortunate enough to live out the dreams that I had as a child.

When I was twelve years old, I remember telling my mom that someday, I would be a pro football player and play in the Super Bowl. I fantasized growing up and moving out to California to live out my dreams.

Remember this always and you too will see, as you read this book that some dreams do come true, if only you believe, work hard and never give up.

People used to say negative things about me. If I got into trouble as a child, there was always that one person that would try to make me feel as though I was nothing.

They would say, "You will never amount to anything!" I never let what people say bother me. I was always a humble person and I have always known who "I" was as a human.

Even as a child, I had full confidence in myself. Never sold myself short or bowed down to the level of those who were jealous of me.

"Believe you me", during my lifetime, I've met my share of several envy-hearted people who would like nothing more than to see me fail.

As I said before, I was always the humble guy and negative words have never taken toll on me or what I believe.

During your lifetime, you must enjoy whatever you do. The whole key to success is the joy and fulfillment that you will receive. This alone is success!

Go about everyday life disassociating yourself with any negativity. I remember my grandfather telling me that I should never speak "things" into existence.

I couldn't fully comprehend this as a kid, but now I understand and appreciate those powerful words. Thank you granddaddy. He has long since past but he will live forever in my memories.

Always keep in mind to never let go of your dreams. Put your focus on a goal and strive to reach it, letting nothing stand in your way. And of course the great men whom we idolize have had to fight and struggle to become the men that they are.

To develop the power of positive thinking is an awesome challenge. But to achieve that power makes use of those positive thoughts and make them realities.

This positive thinking gives you a more upbeat attitude when you are out there on the field.

God gives us powers that help us to evolve into better people. And when we apply positive thinking, it automatically makes us better individuals. So, if we spread positive thinking to those whom are negative, then we have sowed our seeds!

I have always had this strange feeling that when different people are around you, there can be many different attitudes, outlooks, be it positive or negative.

I have forever tried to instill positive influences on any and everybody. By doing this, makes for a positive career, both mentally and physically as well.

Negative influences are not good. These negativity influences will pull you down in ways that you aren't aware.

Stay away from negative people. I have an old saying and it goes like this: weed out your garden so that your flowers can bloom. Think about it!

Getting caught up with negative people may cause you to loose your glory. In other words, they can steal your glory! A person's negative attitude towards life can and will rub off on you. Before long, you will begin to have a negative attitude just like them.

We can't always choose the people that we work with, or have to deal with on a daily basis so therefore, you must stay focused. Keep a positive outlook on everything that you are involved with. Don't let other steal your glory.

I say that because once you become a negative person, this can and will get in the way of your success. Stay positive!

Staying focused doesn't mean that you have to totally abandon the negative crowd. This simply means that you should try spreading a little positive spirit on them. This is called in the eyes of the Lord, "sowing seeds". You will reap harvest from it someday!

Jealous people definitely have a negative outlook on life. That's why it is best that you steer clear of the people that do not want you to succeed. There again, stealing your glory!

Stealing your glory makes them happy. They are jealous because they may not be as good at one thing or another. Or they simply like being alone. If you notice, most jealous people either stick close to other jealous people or they are alone most of the time. That's because no one wants to be around people like that.

Most lonely people are miserable. They bring this on themselves because of their negative attitudes! It kind of goes in a circle.

There are many obstacles that will come in the way of your success. There are more than just negative people; there can be negative places too.

Negative places such as a place where trouble lies. There simply isn't a good way to explain why and where you should be. I can only suggest that you use your common sense and keep your goals on the top of your head at all times.

Thinking about your goals can really help to keep you focused. By doing this, it can bring you that much closer to becoming successful.

Sometimes we have to fight to stay away from these negative forces. It isn't easy at times, but you should spread positive feedback to cushion the blow while you destroy weeds from the garden.

Understand that there is a tough road that you must travel in order to make the dreams that you dream come true, so, be prepared to work hard. Not just the physical aspect, but the mental as well.

Know who you are as a person. Find joy and fulfillment in whatever you dream, remember, dreams do come true, I am living proof.

Being confident in yourself is one of the most important things that you must remember. Not only in athletics, but also in your day to day life situations.

Oftentimes, people treat one another the way that they are treated. This has a lot to do with the way that they were reared. The way that you were brought up has an awful lot to do with your attitude as an adult.

Living a negative lifestyle doesn't have to continue throughout the rest of your days, make a change. This positive or negative attitude has made many great athletes become legends or statistics.

Remember that the price for success is quite expensive. Be prepared to pay whatever the cost may be, while keeping your dignity and self-respect.

You must understand from the very beginning, each and every one of you who wish to become professional athletes, need to start a pattern with the way you go about each and every day of your life.

Patterns that form the way you can and will live for the rest of your life. This pattern is, to sum it all up, all of the things that I have mentioned thus far.

Making good grades, being a good citizen, being a team player and spreading a positive attitude to those that are negative. All of these examples will give you great attributes to become the great person that you are destined to be.

All of the things that are taught to you at a very young age by your parents and by other people who care about you will leave a profound impression on your mind .These great role models will assist you in making the right decisions in the future.

Expectations

I mentioned earlier that football players were, in many ways considered special individuals. They are given special privileges and are expected to always do things in abundant and extreme measures.

Throughout the history of football, the players minds were unknowingly trained to live and abide by a set of rules, a lifestyle, a predetermined reputation set by the players that preceded us.

I say that it is a form of psychological manipulation because having experienced the life of a professional football player; I truly believe that we were brain washed to a degree.

Not so much in the negative sense, because after all, this is what made our lives easier than the average, regular person, but in a way that often did more harm than good in certain aspects of our lives.

You will understand once you read how the National Football League has been indirectly responsible for the failure of many good men.

Politics! That is one heck of a word. It plays a large role in all sports and in each and every one of our lives. Maybe, just maybe, you don't realize at the time, but trust me, you and I deal with politics on a daily basis.

For as long as I can remember playing the game, we were taught that we were above the average. We were to be tough and take nothing that anyone had to offer that we didn't want.

Naturally, we were treated special even by those that we rejected ... tough like a brick wall.

Not only coaches, but the fans as well as the communities that we represent instill in football players that nothing should be able to stand in the way of a true football player. Like a brick wall, not penetrable, and able to take a body punch from a steel ball. Tough as a brick wall and hard as steel.

The mentality of the coaches is to push you as an athlete to the farthermost point that you can physically go. They put in your mind that you can go farther than you think.

The coaches help you to train your mind as well as to train you for what is ahead for you on the football field.

A basketball players' stance is important to a football player. Sounds funny?

They teach you to condition yourself so you are concerned with the outcomes.

Hard work and dedication makes up a good athlete. The coaches drive you to the limit, in all aspects to become a pro.

Part of conditioning comes, pain. All the way back, as far as junior high, the football coach's would give us salt tablets if we were cramping. I had a serious problem cramping on the field.

They wouldn't give you water, but the salt tablets instead. This was a terrible thing for me because I hated to take those salt tablets.

Pain makes you strong in the long run, but while enduring that pain, you might think that it is the worst thing in the world, which, although it may hurt and you wouldn't wish it on your worst enemy, it plays a positive role for you in the future.

This makes one stronger and able to tolerate the torture that sometimes is placed on you out there on the field. As you know, too much salt causes more cramping. You do the math!

Just for your personal information, potassium is what you need for cramps. Bananas are a good source of potassium. Drinking Gatorade will replenish the fluids that have left the body.

Where most average men have the desire to have one woman, a football player was almost expected to play the field and have two or three women. Often times, more than three... orgies.

The media has told the public, that the life of a professional athlete is full of glitz and glamour. Sure, the money is good, if you are good! But, they neglected to tell you the whole story in the truthful version.

Always keep in mind that everything has a price and someone must pay the cost. Sometimes the fee is extremely expensive.

Notice that not everyone is as popular as the next. That's why not all contracts are written the same, so don't expect the unexpected.

Being a team player is very important, not only in sports but, in everything that you do, if it involves others. No team will tolerate anything less

If you are strong and positive and sincere about reaching the goal in which you desperately desire, then, buckle down and condition yourself both mentally and physically as well.

I have been seen and lived a life that is sure to convince you of the fact that professional sports, in general is not all what it is cracked up to be.

I'll show you what all of this means as you enter the part of my life when I turned pro. All of this is a major factor in almost every professional ball player.

I can only ask that you be the judge and jury of us, because before this book is over, you'll some come to realize that it not all that you hear or might see.

If you are someone who has hopes and dream of becoming a professional football player, read between the lines and hear my story. Be prepared to ride a monster of a roller coaster!

Let me make myself clear. I'm not writing this book to belittle myself or anyone else for that matter. Nor is the purpose of this book to have any negative reflecting towards The National Football League from a professional point of view.

The sole reason that I wrote this book is to vent. Writing this was my form of therapy. I needed to express myself in an open manner in order to relieve a lot of built up anger, tension and to share my joys.

I would also like to get a message to all young people out there who have fantasies of a football career that is seen through rose colored glasses.

I say this with all sincerity and from my heart.

FOOTBALL STRATEGIES

Part of a coach's strategies for his team is to motivate each player to a point of changing his attitude to a sense of total control. Meaning that the player should feel that they are indestructible and that nothing can stand in his or her way. Attitude changes to portray greatness.

Each coach has his own way of motivating his team. Some coaches use a phrase or nickname, such as "Let's move it girls!" or "Ladies get your dress tails out of your butt!"

Being given a certain name and hearing it called out when you're pushing yourself, makes one feel that he is doing just a little extra work. This is only a psychological tactic but has been known to be affective.

As in my high school, we were trained to hopefully get the opportunity to be with the "Mighty Five", which was the starting line-up. This was an opportunity that each player wanted in my high school.

Also, each coach has his own personal attitude in which to instill a positive outcome on a player. Some coach may portray a tough and mean attitude. Some may be influential with words of wisdom. This will depend on the coach's personal demeanor.

I can say from experience that coaching, at a high school coach, a college coach and a professional coach all differ in many ways.

Naturally all coaches ultimate goal is to win but there were many differences to me when I played. That's just my own personal opinion, but I feel that each sector has a different strategy and a different goal.

But, every coach that I have known will forever try to get the most out of a player, by any means necessary.

The mentality of every coach is for you to expect to have to do more than the average person. They expect that you always give 200%, at practice and more importantly during each game.

As I mentioned earlier in this book, I felt that the stance of a basketball player (guard) and his gracefulness was helpful to my progress as a good football player. (I played guard when I was into basketball.) And it is another quality that a cornerback and a linebacker needs in order to be able to cover his target.

The coordination that a basketball player needs to be successful is just as important to a football player. He needs the agility and skills to move quickly on his feet while still bouncing the ball.

But for a football player, instead of bouncing the ball, the coordination takes place when one can do the job that the team requires, (blocking, tackling, or running the ball) and the the entire team keep their eyes on the football. Same difference!

Just as on a basketball court, some of the same strategies apply. The games may be different, but the same concept of winning is the main idea.

A good athlete in general, must have good vision and good hearing abilities.

Be able to see your opponent with your peripheral vision. Hear him as well to give you that extra edge and the ups on that player. Brushing up on eye coordination and your hearing skills will be an added plus to you performance.

From a linebacker's point of view, the man who is able to take on two or more blockers will be far more successful than a blocker who can handle only one man. This is really common sense!

This was one quality that I possessed. I had the ability to take and sit down three or more opponents!

In addition to the force behind my attack, this made me stand out from many of the other great players who were just as good but didn't try to handle more than one or two men.

Politics!

Being a linebacker, I always liked being one on one, man to man and man on man. I would hold onto my target and did whatever it took to take that man down. I had great coverage from all angles on the field. This attribute made me one of the great player's.

From the viewpoint at field level, there are many things that make a certain player better than you. For instance, one player might be quicker than you are, or one might hit just a little harder than you.

This should not deter you from learning from your faults, but from the strengths of others. Those that are strong in certain areas also must have a weak area.

I took the opportunity when I played to focus and study the next guys form and style of play. This enabled me to become stronger in my weak point before my weaknesses were even noticed.

It took a lot of trials and errors before *I* became strong in certain areas, but it paid off once I got on the field and went head on against the stronger guy.

What I'm trying to say is, just because a player might seem to be better than you are, take advantage of his strong points and turn your weak point into strong ones.

This not only applies to football, because this strategy works in all aspect of life.

I also learned from many years on the field that investigating a player's family background, personality and strategies on and off the field worked to my advantage. This aided in my becoming such a success on and off the field.

To be able to understand the coaches was a major plus on my performance on the football field too. Being able to understand exactly what a coach expected from you as a player and not just being a player acting for himself.

Let's say that a certain coach has a personality complex with a player that gives up. That would make that coach angry and this will cause verbal outbreaks from that coach. To avoid that, I would always put forth 200% effort. This pleased that particular coach.

Or if a coach is one, that like's to instill words of confidence and encouragement; I would always listen with both ears as well as consume the material that he was speaking.

Just by having my undivided attention will cause him to have just a little more respect for me than if one of my teammates shrugged him off as being an old pesky man.

These are all simple, yet common sense techniques that will work in you favor. And I'm sure that you will learn something from each instance and/or situation. I did!

Younger athletes are big and strong. They tend to be stronger and able to outrun the next player. Hard work and focusing on your goals along with these positive attributes as a young player will help your development into becoming a fine professional athlete for many years to come.

This is not to say that an older pro player is slower or weaker than the younger guy. This just explains what individuality means to an old or young player.

A player must want to do what he does. He has to have a burning desire to become an outstanding player.

Even if he is good but has no fire and desire, he will not shine as the Star that could be deep down inside of him. You have to love the sport and all that comes with it in order to be successful.

If you look at all of the hard work that you are putting into perfecting your position, then understand that it takes this and a whole lot more to reach that goal that you have set for yourself.

But if you just work hard and don't have 100% of your heart into it, then this is working in vain and working for nothing really and truly!

All of these things and many more aid in making football strategies work in their favor.

Let's keep in mind that not all athletes will make it to the pros. But if you focus on making your skills the best that you can give, then being a great high school player will lead you to earning a scholarship to a fine college.

Although you may have hopes of becoming a professional football player, a good education and a college degree will prove to be just as rewarding.

Especially if one receives a scholarship, this would be wonderful because the average college tuition is oftentimes the same as what my parents' paid for their entire house and property way back then.

Let's just say that hard work and dedication is extremely economically correct.

My older brothers had to work hard to put themselves through college and I know that this had to be awfully hard on him and his family.

But thank God he made it and didn't get distracted by all of the temptations that we often see throughout our lifetimes.

Sure, professional athletes have a great image and may luck up and get a contract that will be financially positive, but to have an education is far more priceless than the fame and glory.

And then if you get blessed to have both, a college degree and a professional contract, well let's just say that you are truly blessed.

Then, you should thank the almighty God because there are thousands of athletes that don't even get the opportunity to get a scholarship. There are those who may be good, but opportunity just passed right by them.

I say all of this to make a point, always expect the worst but pray for the best.

God forbid, a player has an accidental injury in the middle of his college career. Then without an education, what's he to do to earn finances for him and his family?

That's why it is important to always have something to fall back on.

Putting forth your extreme efforts in your scholastic abilities is just as important as focusing and working hard at the sport that you pray for success in.

Knowing why you do what you do, be it football, basketball, tennis or even chess, and understanding why you do it is very important!

And realize that no one is forcing you to go out there and do what you do. Participating in a sport is an elective and not something that is required. Therefore, know what and why you do the things that you do. This will also help you to better your skills in the chosen field.

It has always been said that some athletes have tunnel vision. This means that they only see straight ahead and their minds and eyes don't actually see what might distract them from the desired success.

It also means that a player only concentrates on the sport and nothing else. Not a good idea! Not only in football, but, in all of life's situations, please, always have a backup plan.

Keep in mind, football is not a sport that you can play all of your life. With time, we grow old. As we grow old, our bodies tend to weaken. Our minds are not as sharp and neither are our reflexes.

Plus, keep in mind that there are many, many other athletes just waiting to take your place with that team that you are a part of.

Take it from me, a country boy from Evans Hills in the heart of the small town called Fayetteville, North Carolina. I know that opportunity can easily pass you right over. I was truly blessed to be given all of the opportunities that I was given.

I was blessed with these things because, I worked hard at the sport and I focused on the goals that I had set long before as a child.

I always tried to listen to my elders and I tried awfully hard to do the right things on and off of the field. I suggest that you do the same if your dream is to become a reality.

Staying focused and trying to always do the right things in life can get pretty hard at times, but if your EXPECTATIONS are to become a successful professional athlete, then tell yourself, 'Nothing is too hard. Succeeding the hardships will make me strong'!

From my point of view, today, there are fewer great

White football athletes than blacks.

Let's face it, there is a greater number of African American, professional football players. Ask yourself why?

Could it be because the whites are not as gifted in the physical sense or they do not care anymore.

Maybe it's because they are sometimes forced by their parents to play ball and maybe this attributes to the fact that they don't give it their all while playing!

Quite possibly they don't put into the game 100% because they don't like the sport and only play because of their family history.

Most black athletes tend to give more than 100% of themselves because they feel that they have something to prove.

Oftentimes, a black athlete may feel that it is expected of them to be great on the football field or basketball court.

It is not a proven fact, but takes a look at what the history book tells and shows us.

Society has bestowed in us that all black men are good athletes. Is this true? Of course not, there again, politics have come into play! Politics of our society as we see it today!

Desire is something that we must have on the inside and you must have it in order to want to give that 200% that it takes to make that one great play or to be that top executive.

ARE YOU READY TO BE A PRO?

I know that there are hundreds of thousands of people, who wish to become professional athletes, but there is a lot that is required to reach that point.

If you look through the history of time, you will see that all of those who have reached the point of stardom, worked extremely hard. The kind of hard work that requires that each and every waking moment is spent either thinking or practicing or conditioning one's body.

Unless you are one of the luckiest people on earth to be born with the skills that are required to reach the point of being a household name, then I sure hope that you are prepared for each and every day of your life thinking, practicing and conditioning yourself.

Doing these things, so that you will stand out and be noticed over all of the thousand of people who have devoted their life to reach that point.

Not only training you body, but training your mind as well. This is just as important as being fit physically.

There are at least forty-five players that make up a complete football team. And in the professional league, there are only, maybe seven stars that come out of the season.

The five or so that do make it to be the top players will probably have enough finances to retire on. Then, you must ask yourself, what happens to the rest of the players and their future, for themselves and for their families?

In the beginning a player is given a standard contract. A contract that is, healthy enough to purchase a nice house and car. After that large sum is gone, then what?

The average fan, don't know all of the tricks and trades that the N. F. L. has in store for a potential good athlete.

The public only knows what the media presents via newspapers, television and advertisements. The truth is shaded by a life that is full of glitz and glamour!

It's not told of what becomes of a player if something should happen to that player physically.

I mean, say for instance that a player was the star on his college or high school team, (there are some players who are good enough to go straight from high school to the pros), and he or she lands a contract for say, *2.5* million dollars.

The lifestyle that a professional athlete needs to live up to, per the media, is extravagant, correct?

Well, most athletes try to live up to the lifestyle that the last or former athlete lived. You know, a large house in the finest of neighborhoods, Mercedes Benz or Hummer, the best of expensive furniture and then, he has to look the part, that is as far as clothes are• concerned. As we all know, Gucci, Dolce Gabana and Evisu, etc... are very expensive! Am I correct?

Well, that wraps up well over half the salary, especially when that 'star' as they want to be called, has to pamper and dress and fix it so that his or her spouse is up to par as well, correct?

Now then, if you lived to that extreme, just exactly how long do you think that, that little money will last? No longer than a year, two tops!

Now, let's say that, God forbid, he or she has an injury that prohibits them from playing for the duration of the season. Where do you think they are headed?

Especially when the N. F. L. realizes that they are out of 2.5 million dollars and are left without their " Star". How

Do you think they will handle that?

They have to renegotiate the players' contract. Keep in mind that they do have their "tails" covered somewhere in the original contract!

And for the N. F. L. to negotiate a contract means that if a player doesn't, play in at least six games, then the league can, have and will simply tear up your contract!

If a player does play in at least six games with or without injury then the N. F. L. is required to pay only half of the salary that is stated on that contract.

So, at any given time, a player is not secure with a contract. Not by the National Football League standards!

If they didn't cover themselves, then they would be giving money away, with many prayers that their "Star" will last through out their expensive contract. If they didn't then the N. F. L. would have gone bankrupt long, long ago.

Say that player is good enough to make the team, but isn't good enough to be the 'star'. Well, that player would naturally receive a contract for a lesser amount of salary.

Well, ask yourself, if the money isn't invested properly, how long do you feel that the player will be able to afford the lifestyle in which the media portrays that a professional athlete leads? Not long at all!

Then, what about their families and their financial retirement situation? Doesn't seem too pretty do it?

These are only a few of the things that a person should train his or her mind for! And now, what about the physical training?

Believe you me, the physical aspect is far more important! One must be cautious of injuries. This is one of the most important things to consider when one signs a contract. A contract that he or she must live up to.

Not only because of contractual and financial reasons, but for health reasons more importantly!

None of us anticipates having an injury, but face it, they do happen. Maybe not because of something you did wrong, but because of the laws of gravity.

Maybe your body turns wrong or you fall in a difficult manner and break a bone, or fracture one. Maybe you tear a tendon, or whatever may cause one to be sidelined or benched.

These things do happens, even though we hope and pray that they don't, but what would then become of your career?

Many of these things are not thought of by someone who dreams of becoming the next household name in sports, but they should be thought of and more emphasis should be placed on finding the right person or firm to negotiate one's contract. This firm or person is called an "agent". That alone requires investigations and probing into.

To find a good agent, one must, first of all, find out what is in it for them and why they feel that they can help you.

Many times, an athlete automatically assume that, if someone or some firm tells them that the earth is square and this sounds good to them, then that athlete will believe in that firm or person and indirectly will place his or her future in the hands of what could possibly be the devil.

One must search and inquire about the person or firm that her or she is interested in and probe for the truth in their history behind their own career as an agent.

Once you have found that special agent, then you must find a good attorney to follow behind them. I know this seems like a lot of unnecessary work if that firm or person has all of the right credentials.

But, trust me; these details must be explored if the player wants what is in his or her best interest.

I'm certain that in all of our lifetimes, we have come across many that didn't have our best interest at heart. Then, when choosing someone that will have your entire future in their hands, please, take my advice and dig deep into their past.

Their future may tell you what if any trust can or should be instilled with them. This is really common sense, but a lot of times, we all may tend to block out the sun to feel the rain, understand?

Okay, now, say that a player is one of the five stars on that team. And let's say that they get a contract for say, 15 million dollars and he of course must live to the extreme, the extreme life of a multi-millionaire. This naturally will cause him or she to shell out, far more than the average millionaire, am I correct?

Alright, now, let's say that the lifestyle that the media puts out for a person of this financial magnitude is so grand that some of you can't possibly think of enough ways to spend it all.

If that "Star" doesn't get the big head with arrogance to the point that they mess up all of that money and doesn't invest into a potential profit gaining investment, then you do the math, what then?

HONOR TO MY COACHES

We had a football team in which I played linebacker. E. E. Smith recruited me from Washington Drive. This is the beginning of the story that tells you of the legendary Joe Harris, also known as the "Stud".

I really felt honored and proud as a sophomore to play with the varsity high school team as a starter. And I enjoyed this immensely.

To name a few of our coaches that we had throughout my high school, they were: Coach Bishop Harris, Coach William Carver, Coach Duck Carter and Ike Walker.

Coach Bishop Harris was the most motivational coach that I have ever had the pleasure of knowing throughout my entire career.

He was the one that always thought that a football player should have more than one of everything.

Two or more girls, two or more beers or two or more of what ever: with hopes that your are able to endure more than the average!

Coach William "Bill" Carver was the man who taught me to be challenging. He would put the five toughest guys on the front line. We were called the "Mighty Five"!

Coach Duck Carter was a man of medium height, bald headed and mean as a hornet! Somewhat called the brains of the operation for the "Mighty Golden Bulls" at E. E. Smith High School. He was the best at putting together an offensive football strategy that was sure to please any crowd.

But the man that helped me most of all was the uncle of my best friend, Charlie Baggett and his name was Coach Ike Walker.

This was a man of distinct character. A tall man, of about 6"2". He was not the one of our football coaches, but he was the track coach as well as the head coach of the basketball team. He was our defensive coordinator.

Coach Walker taught me the history of the black man and how we contributed to our society as a nation. I really admired his knowledgeable tactics when getting his point across to us.

I would like to say a special thank you to this man... Thank you Ike!

Then there was Coach Kelley. He was my basketball coach along with Coach Walker.

This was a very family oriented man who believed in togetherness. He taught us that there is power in numbers and expressed that we as players must stick together to form a shield of strength!

All of the above were coaches from my high school days.

When I entered college at Georgia Institute of Technology, I found it to be a totally different world outside of Fayetteville, North Carolina.

It was because of their strength, knowledge and wisdom that I found my home away from home at Georgia Tech.

Coach Bud Carson was one of the head coaches.. Then there was Coach Bill Fulcher and Coach Pepper Rogers.

There were a number of assistant coaches: Maxie Baughan, Ken Blair, Jerry Glanville, Floyd Reese, and Lamar Leachman. Sorry to say, Coach Brooks is now deceased.

Jerry Glanville was the Head Coach for the Atlanta Falcons and now is the assistant Coach at University of Hawaii.

He was a funny and tactful man.

Ken Blair is a retired scout for the Atlanta Falcons. He was also at one point in his career a scout for the Denver Broncos.

This is one of the most serious and down to earth coaches that I ever had the opportunity of working with. He helped me to become the number one tackler in the history of Georgia Tech.

Floyd Reese was an astounding assistant coach to me. He was respectful and honest. One of the friendliest coaches ever. He loved me

Lamar Leachman was one of our defensive line coaches. He had lots of funny sayings that stand vivid in my mind. A big man he was!

He retired as the Defensive Line Coach for the New York Giants.

I recall Eddie Robinson, the head coach of Grambling University, asking me in 1971 why I chose to go to a "white" school instead of a black school. My response to him was simple. The black schools only gave me partial scholarships and I would have to work to help pay the tuition. White schools guaranteed me a full scholarship for 4 years that would pay for everything including food and rent.

Special Thanks to: Bud Carson, LA Rams, defensive coordinator, Bud Grant, Head Coach at Minnesota Vikings, George Allen head coach of the Washington Redskins, Don Schula, Miami Dolphins head coach, Ray Malovasi, head coach of the LA Rams, Lionel Taylor (offensive Coordinator),

Dan Radakovich (offensive Line Coach), Herb Paterra (linebacker coach), Paul Lanham (quarterbacks coach), Frank Lauterbur (defensive line coach),

Dennis Green, former head coach of the Arizona Cardinals, Jimmy Ray, wide receiver coach for the NY Jets, John Guy player personnel for Buffalo Bills, Bishop Harris, running back coach of San Francisco 49ers, Charlie Baggett, assistant head coach Miami Dolphins, Pete McCullough, head coach of the San Francisco 49ers and Lawrence Taylor, New York Giants.

My buddies Rod Perry- coach of North Carolina Panthers, Pat Thomas cornerback coach for the Buffalo Bills, Reggie Wilkes, and Anthony Prior.

WHERE ARE THEY NOW?

Today, the most troublesome kid of our group, Arnell McSwain, is living in Tucson, Arizona. He has become a minister.

Then there was my best friend, Charlie Baggett. He went on to try out for The Hamilton Tigercats located in Canada.

Once I was traded to that team, I was able to land him an opportunity at try-outs. He didn't make the team unfortunately, but later became a N. F. L. Coach for several different teams. One hell of a man! Now he is a coach for the Miami Dolphins, wide receiver coach.

Ronnie McDonald is still residing in Fayetteville, North Carolina and working for Kelly Springfield Tire Company.

Jerry Porter and Donald Kelly also became evangelists. Donald lives in Atlanta, Georgia and I'm not quite sure where Jerry lives.

My brother, James was quite good in basketball. After high school, he went on to play for Fayetteville State and there, he earned his business degree. He did really well for himself. He returned to our hometown area and married Ceretta Raines .They had two children, James Jr., we call him Jim and a sweet girl named Karinda. Now he has since retired from Goodyear Tire Company. He was ahead of the minority division of the Human Resources Department with the company. James now resides in Tennessee.

My oldest brother John unfortunately has passed. He was in a motorcycle accident and later, from his wounds developed cancer. Before dying, he married Betty Jo and they bore two children, Debra and Leon. Both kids inherited John's flair for holding encouraging and wise conversation. They got John's energetic personalities as well. Leon was born on the same day that I was born.

Clyde Chessney was one of the first black athletes to come out of Evan Hills. He went to North Carolina State, which is located in Raleigh, North Carolina.

Our old safety back in high school, Dennis Monroe lives here in Atlanta not too far from where I live. Dennis didn't go on to become a pro athlete; instead, he graduated from A & T University in Greensboro, North Carolina. He majored in R.O.T. C. in the Air Force. He later became Major Monroe in the United State Air Force! He now works for the government at Fort McPherson as an Intelligence Information Analyst.Dennis Monroe and I often times get together and rehash some old stories. We have a very good friendship as we've gotten older and I cherish that bond. He's a great guy; one of my best friends today.

Once married to a lovely lady but unfortunately they got a divorce but out of the marriage they had a lovely and smart son named Theus and a daughter named Gabriel. They call me Uncle Joe! Beautiful and intelligent kids. Theus is now a barber and Gabriel is now attending Howard University in Washington, D. C.

UNDERSTANDING GOD

When I was growing up, my mother always insisted that we go to church. She was taught very strict discipline in regards to church going and in the praising of the Lord. This weekly task each Sunday was passed on to us.

We attended a church called John Wesley Methodist Church. Located at the end of Frolic Street, on a hill. The road was nothing but mud and a hill. It was not an easy one to drive up after a good rain.

It was a nice size church, not big, but medium sized. It had a brick front and a large, tall steeple out in front of it.

Our pastor was a humble and solid man who preached his sermon as though it had been rehearsed like a play.

His words will be with me until the day that I die. Although way back then, it really meant little to me. But adulthood and my experiences have made me wise to become closer to my Father in Heaven.

There was a sanctified bible study group that was located out back of the church with a choir director, and she wanted me to join the choir and church band. I played the clarinet as I spoke of earlier, but again, that positively wasn't my forte.

I enjoyed going to church. I did not quite understand the true purpose. It seemed to be a simple ritual. I remember thinking that it helped the time to go by.

Little did I know that those simple weekly visits to the church would have such a profound affect on my life as I live it today.

I knew that there was a God and that we, as Christians honored the Lord and tried, many times without success to obey the Ten Commandments.

But it wasn't until my young adult life that I understood more the true meaning of being a Christian.

I'm a born again Christian now. Although, I was baptized as a kid, being a born again Christian has made a very distinguished and noticeable difference in the way I live and carry myself. It also has made my thoughts and outlook on the right ways of living.., living for the Lord.

When I accepted the Lord as my personal savior, my life changed for the better. I have such a peace of mind that, it sometimes scares me.

Oh, don't get me wrong, it has taken many years and many setbacks to reach the point that I had to find my spirituality. I've probably committed more sins than the good book speaks against.

I'll elaborate more on my atrocities, downfalls and on the wrong choices that I've made in the past later in this book.

There was a time in my life when thoughts and praises to God hardly ever crossed my mind. Although we knew that God was an important factor in our lives, it had little bearing on us as children.

Now, I praise the Lord and I'm so grateful that He has accepted and forgiven my many sins and blesses me each and every day.

We often take for granted the small things or circumstances that we experience. Such as giving thanks to God for awaking us each morning. I'm so much happier with myself, now that I have found Jesus.

I've always been a good, humble and kindhearted person, but during my lifetime, I have done some pretty wild and crazy things. Things that I'm not proud of, but I truly believe that our experience in life, that are placed in or lives are part of the plan that God have chosen for us.

I can say that I honestly believe that things happen for a reason and these obstacles and challenges that we go through make us stronger beings once we find out that the only way to live is the way that Jesus taught and teaches us to be.

I don't know about you, but I plan on going to Heaven! If you don't know by now that He is coming, I suggest that you read your Bible and understand that we are definitely in Revelations. To make it to those pearly gates, you must find Jesus and live His way of life.

I would like to take a moment to thank the Almighty for giving the opportunity to live a life that has been full of experiences that has made me strong and has brought to my attention that nothing is more powerful than His words. Thank you Father for the wisdom that you blessed me with to be as successful as I am.

I also thank you, for the many serious challenges that I faced during my life. For these are the things that have made me appreciate the little things and not to take for granted the fact that we are not promised tomorrow and if it is your will, then it will be done.

Thanks for bringing to this point of peace within myself Father. Understanding what spirituality means and respecting it because it is for and from the Lord is the only reason for all of the successes is what life has to offer and that success what you desire and work so hard for.

Live your life in the godly manner and all of your wishes and dreams will come to be. Study your Bible, pray and believe.   Be Blessed!

Secrets of Success

S – start by determining your ultimate goal in life

E – establish your priorities to reflect those goals

C – create a plan that includes room for flexibility

R – research and practice to reduce risks and errors

E – efforts lead to rewards, excuses lead to failures

T – time used wisely is an investment for the future

S – strength is achieved by confronting difficulties

O – organization, focus, & persistence gain results

F – faith in Jesus frees you from fear and doubt

S – self control is the truest test of human mastery

U – use your talents and skills as natural resources

C – challenges always offer opportunities for growth

C – change is the only constant you should depend on

E – experience exceeds all other methods of learning

S – society never owes you more than you have earned

S – success is a way of life found moment by moment